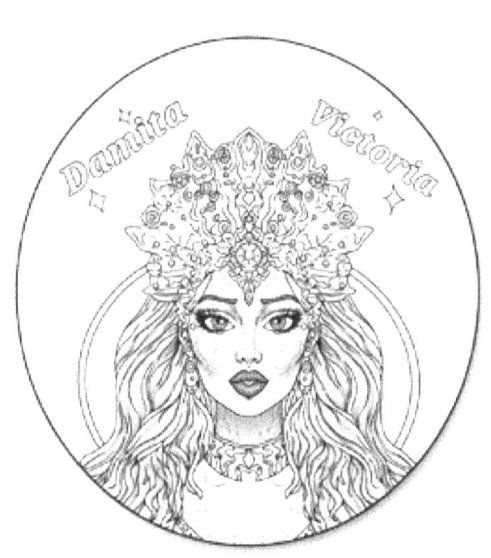

ADULT MANDALA COLORING PAGES
COLORING BOOK FOR ADULTS STRESS RELIEVING DESIGNS

This book belongs to

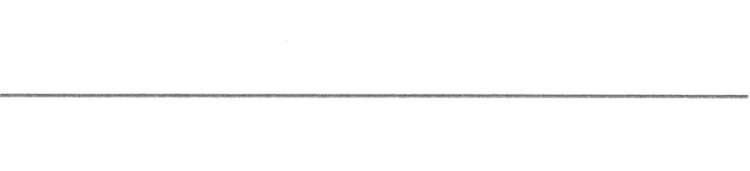

_____

_____

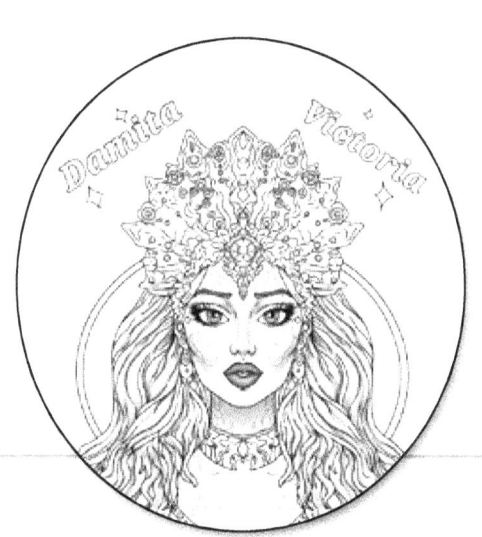

Damita Victoria

COLORING TIPS

We have printed the art in single-sided pages. Each image is placed on its own black-backed page to reduce the bleed-through to the next image.

If you are using markers, it strongly recommended sliding a piece of cardstock or thick paper behind the page you are working on to make sure the ink doesn't stain the next page.

Now Relax and enjoy the "ME" Time

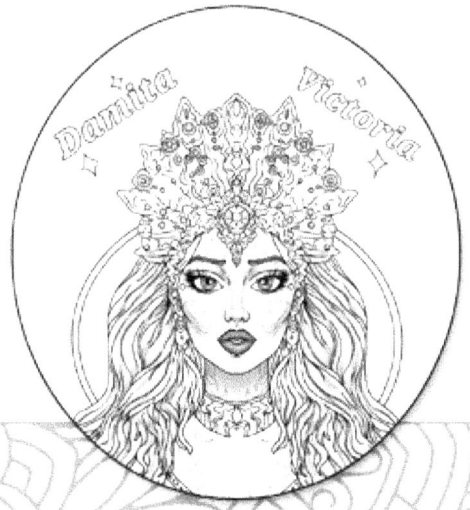

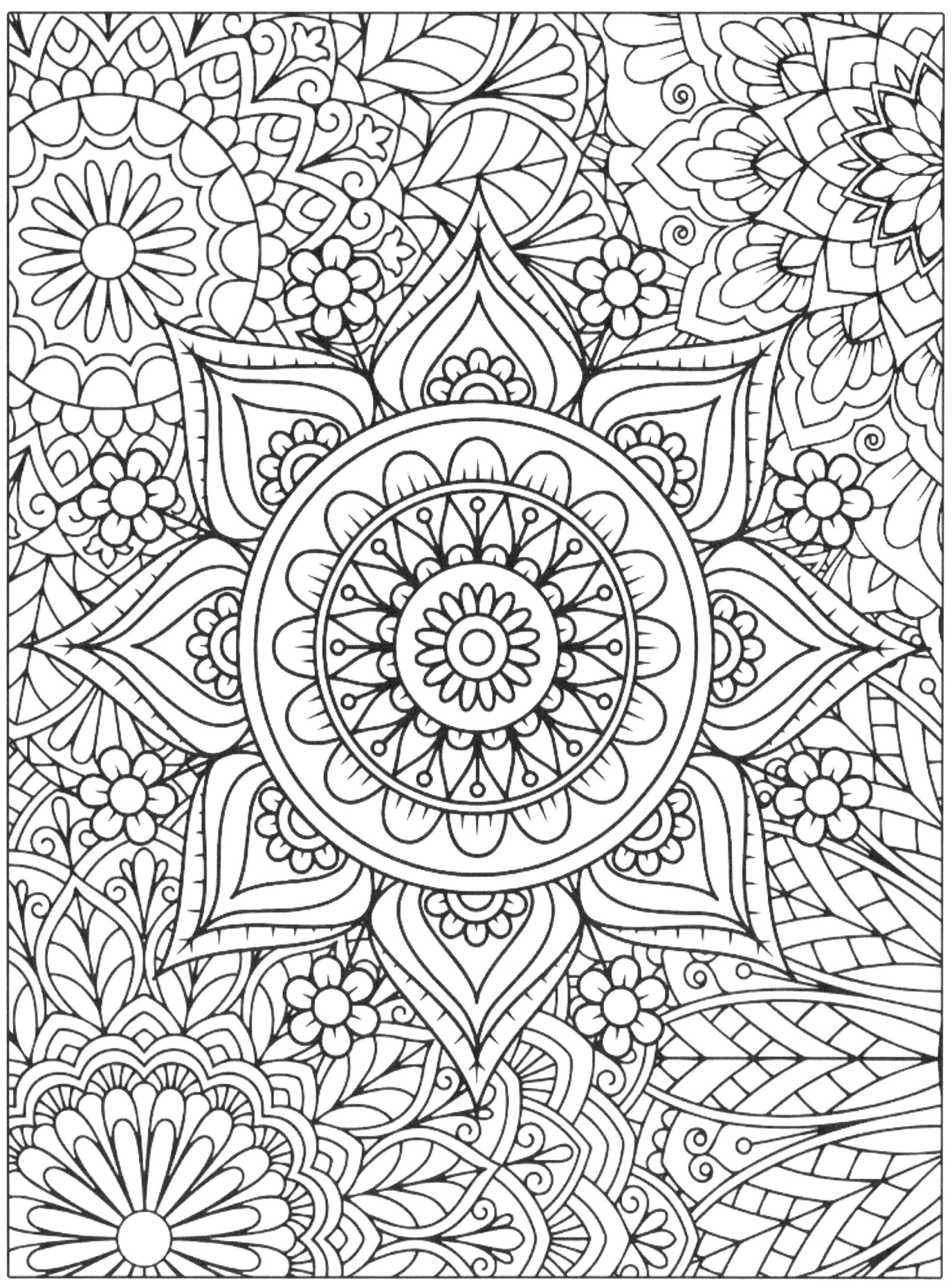

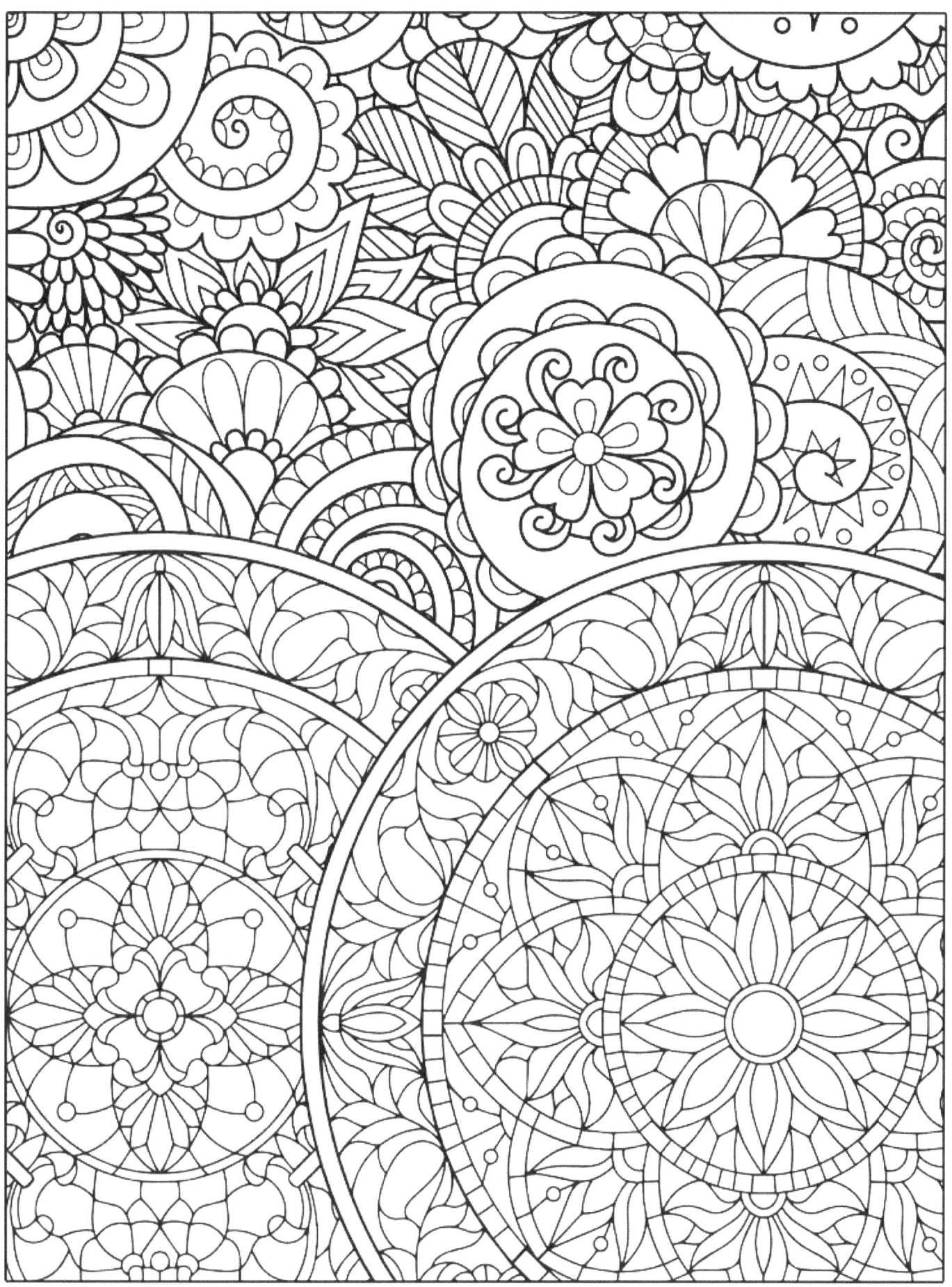

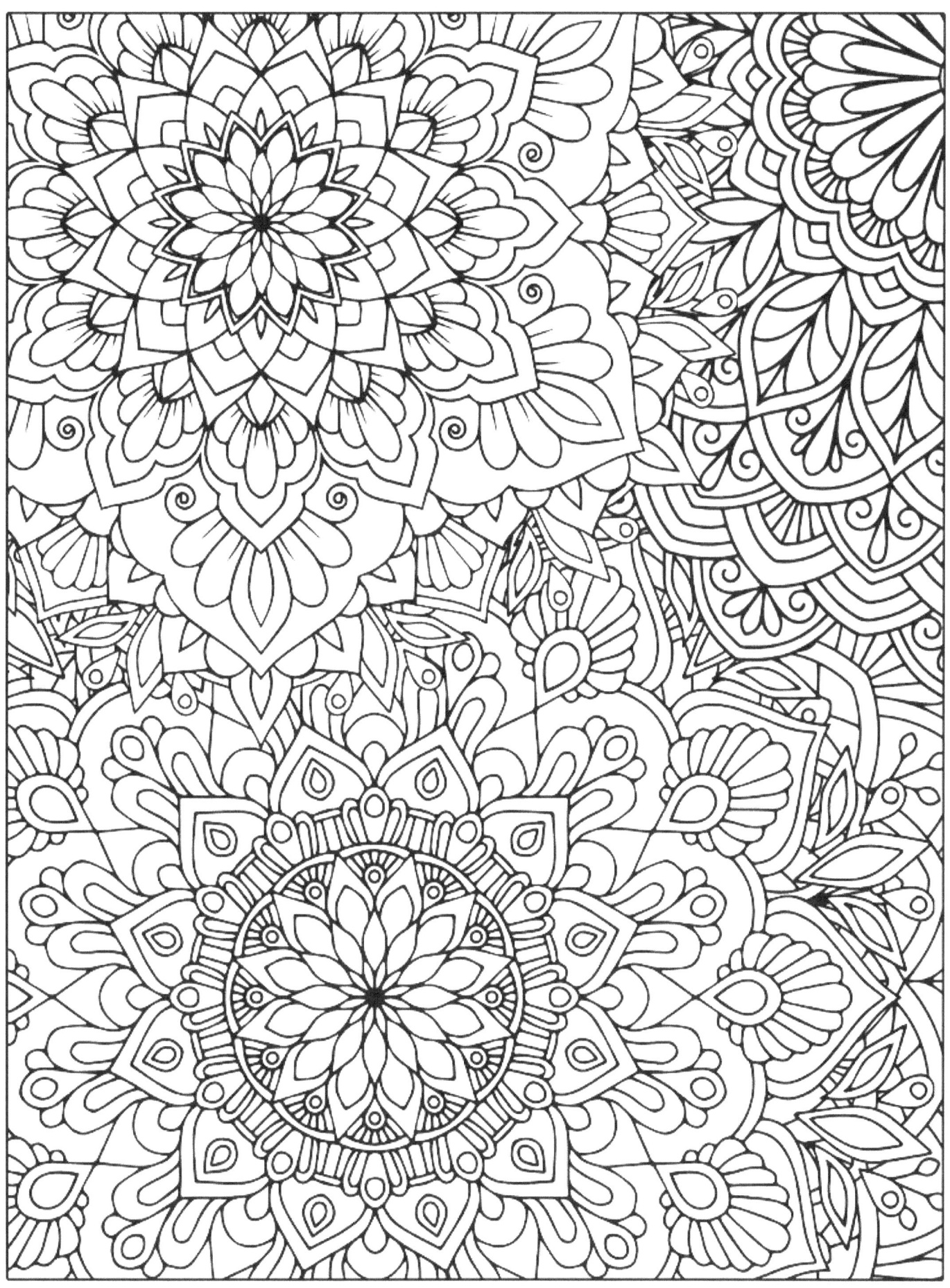

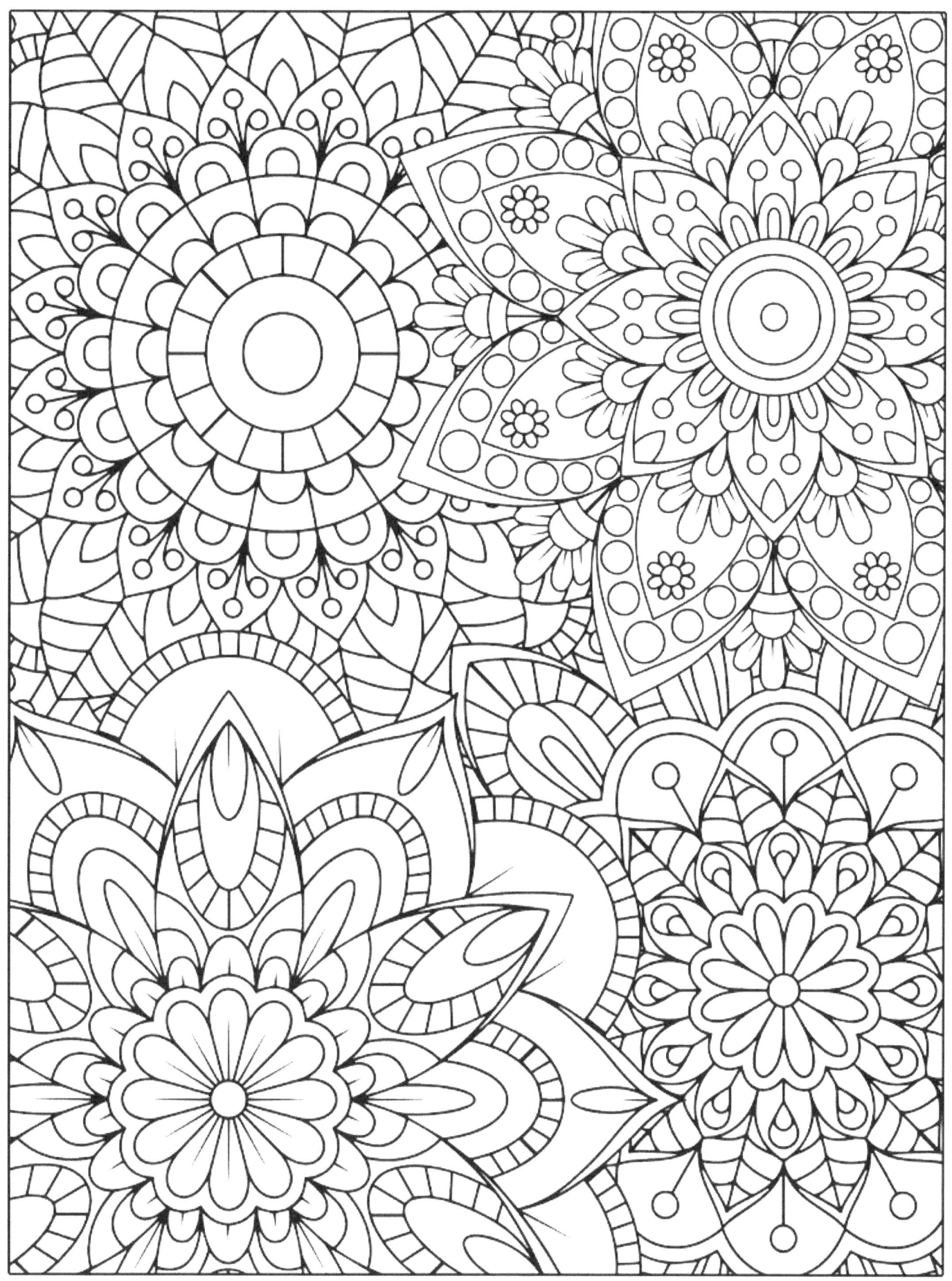

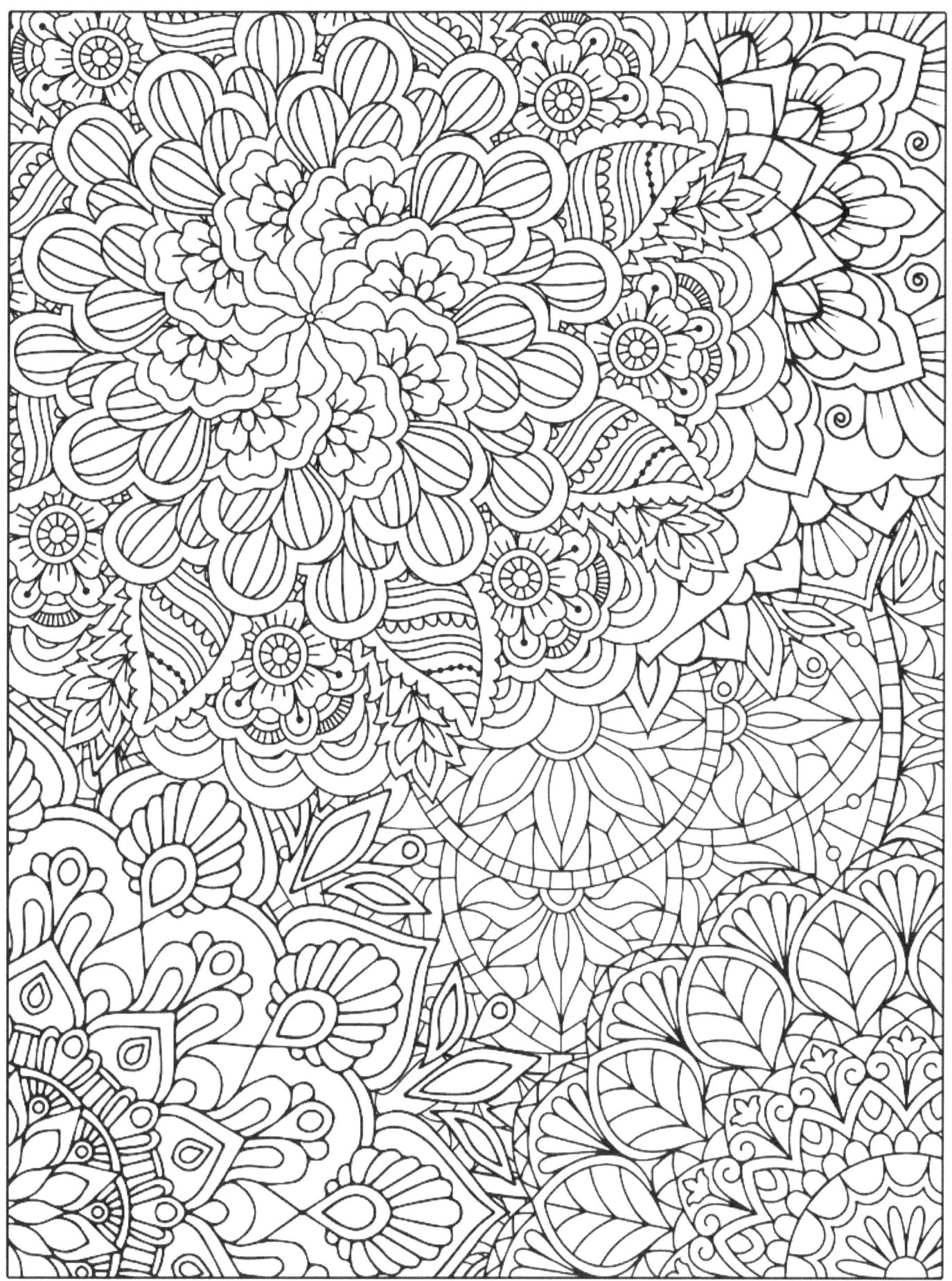

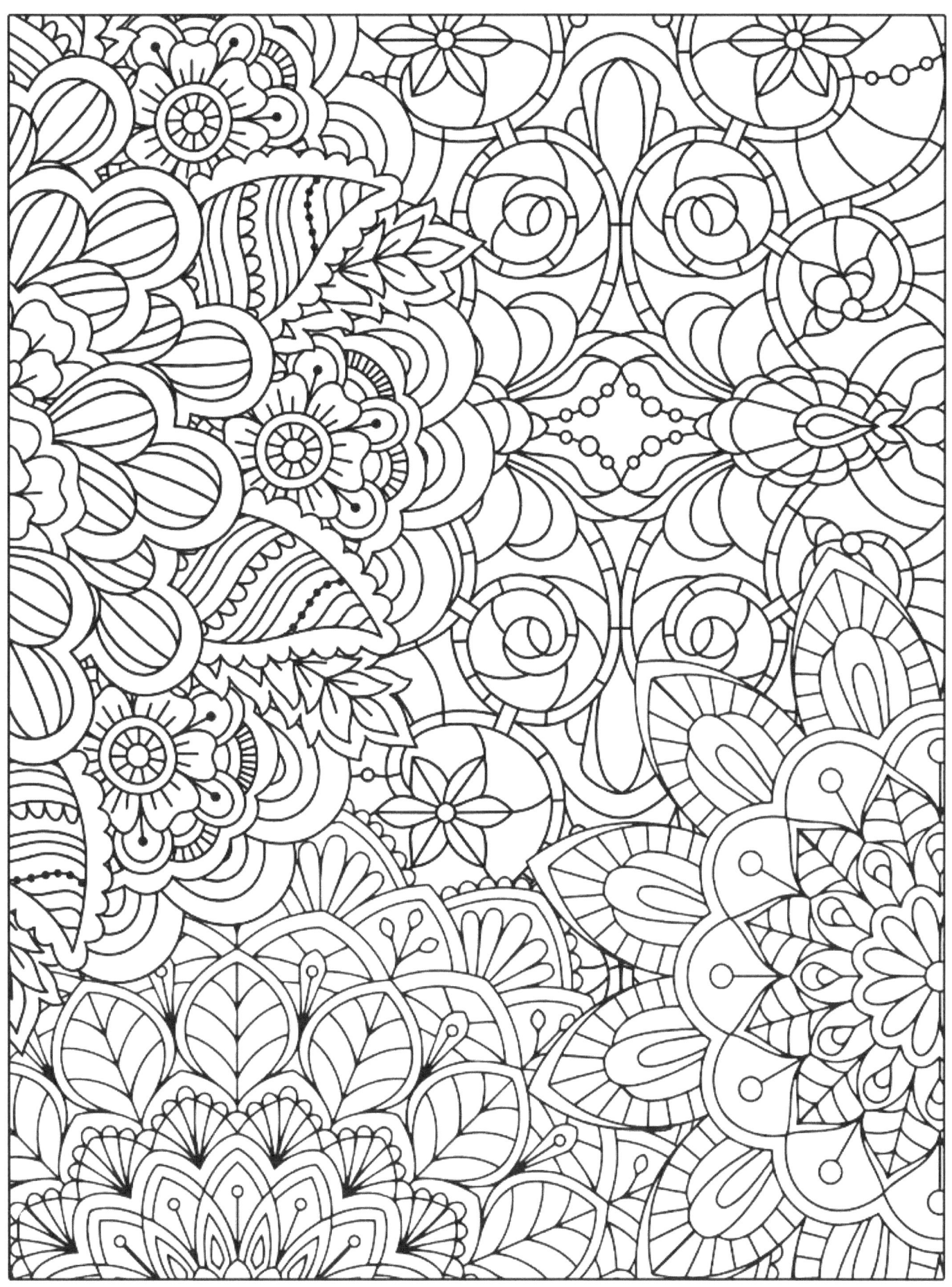

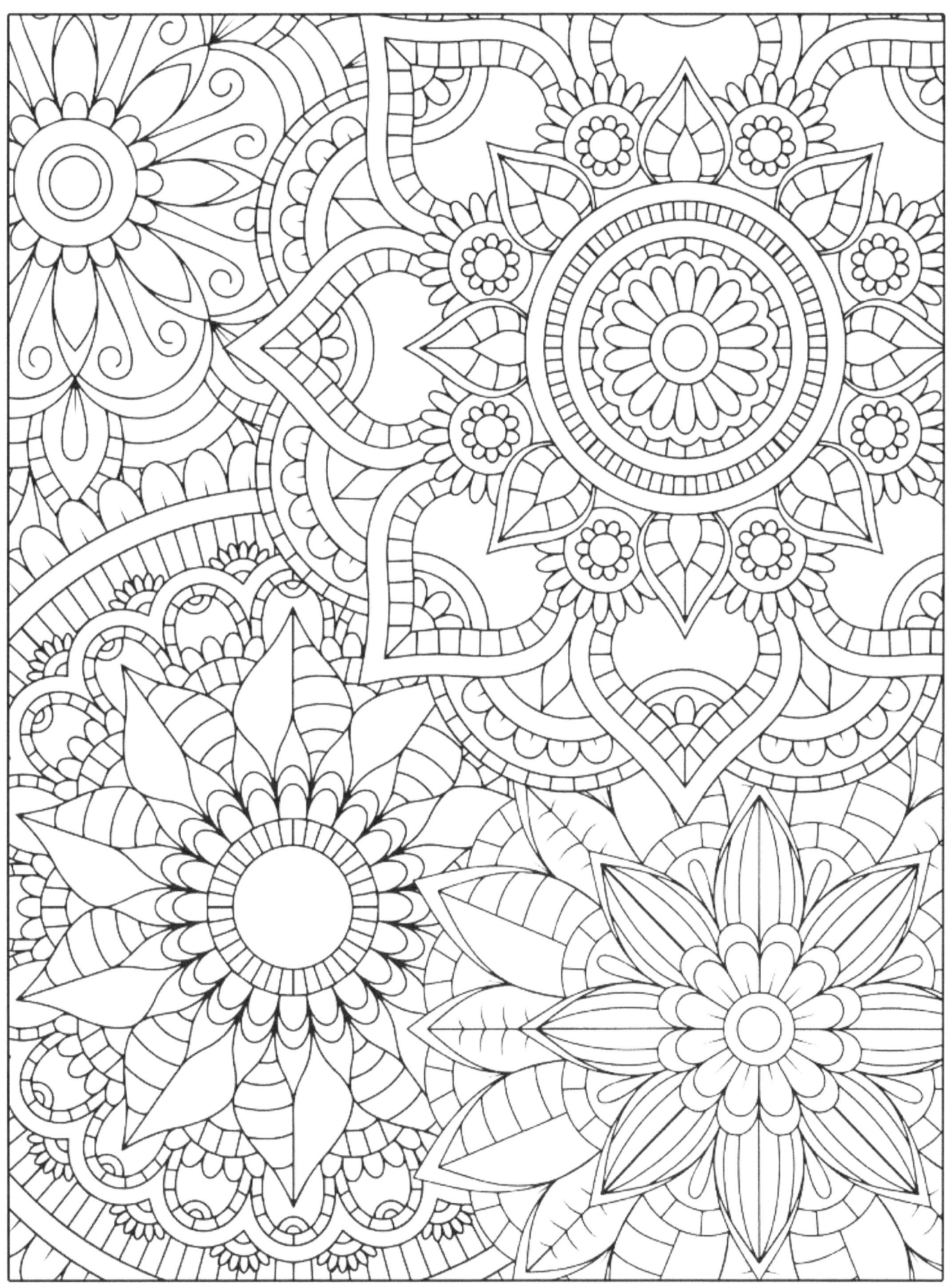

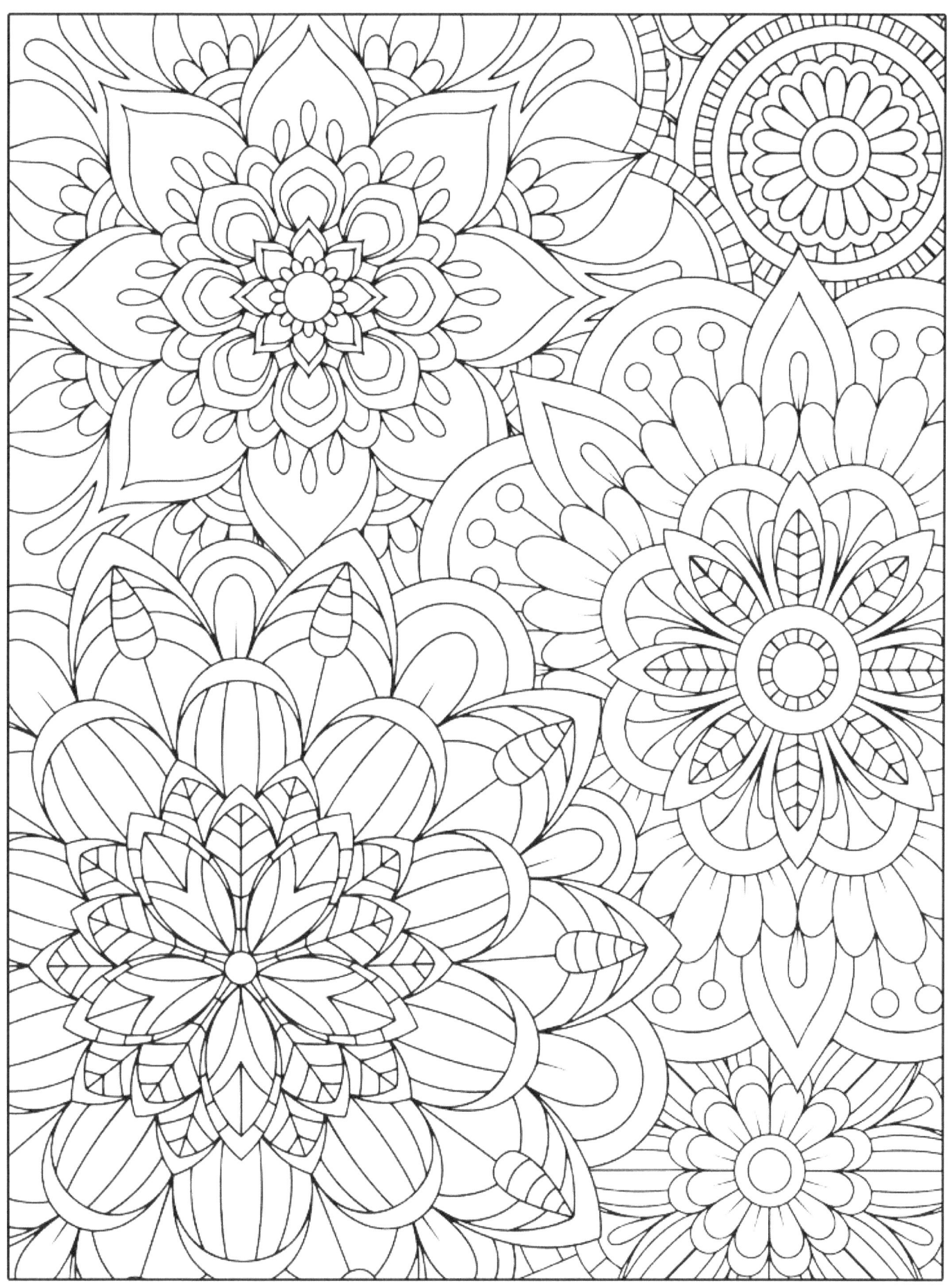

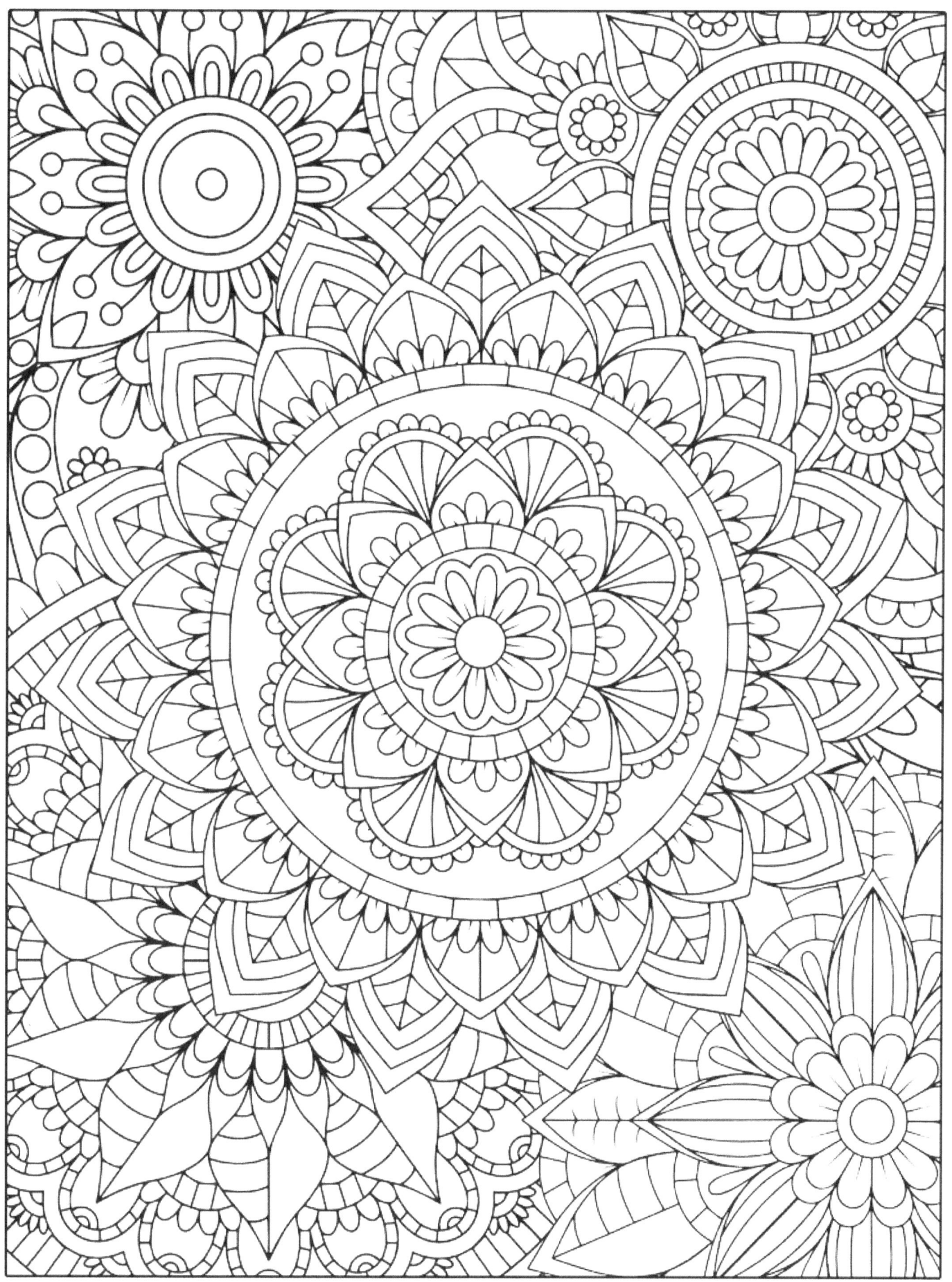

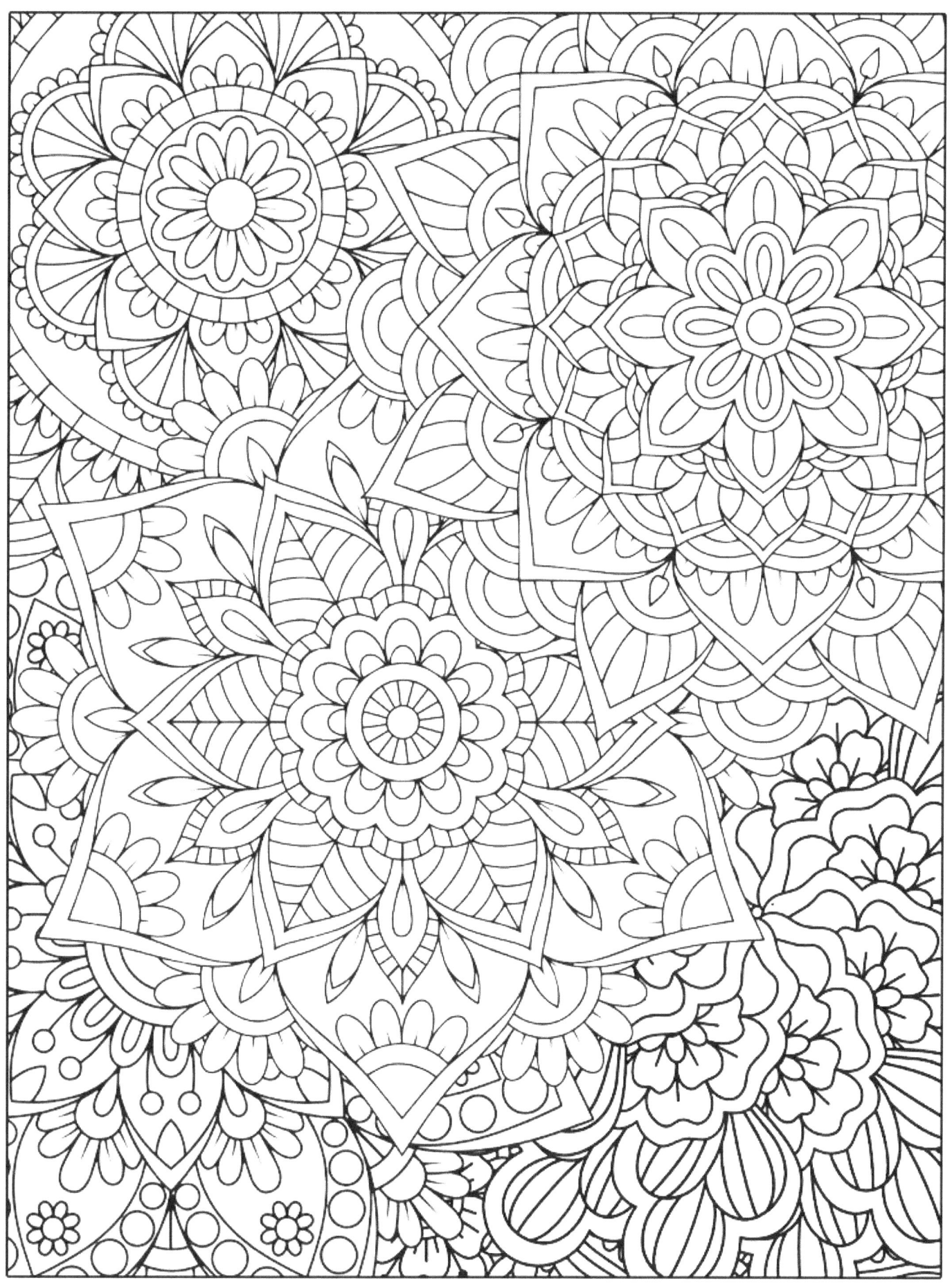

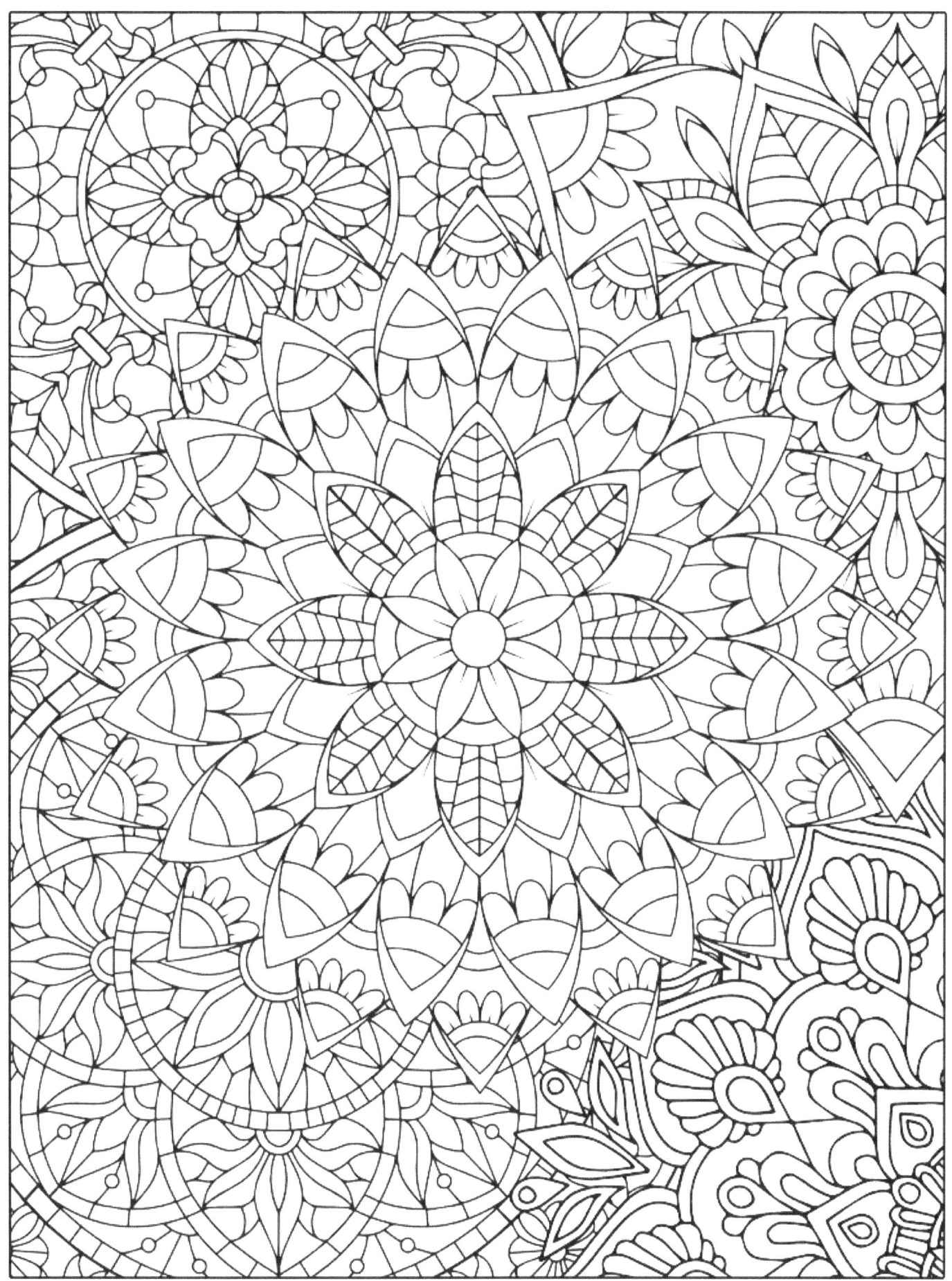

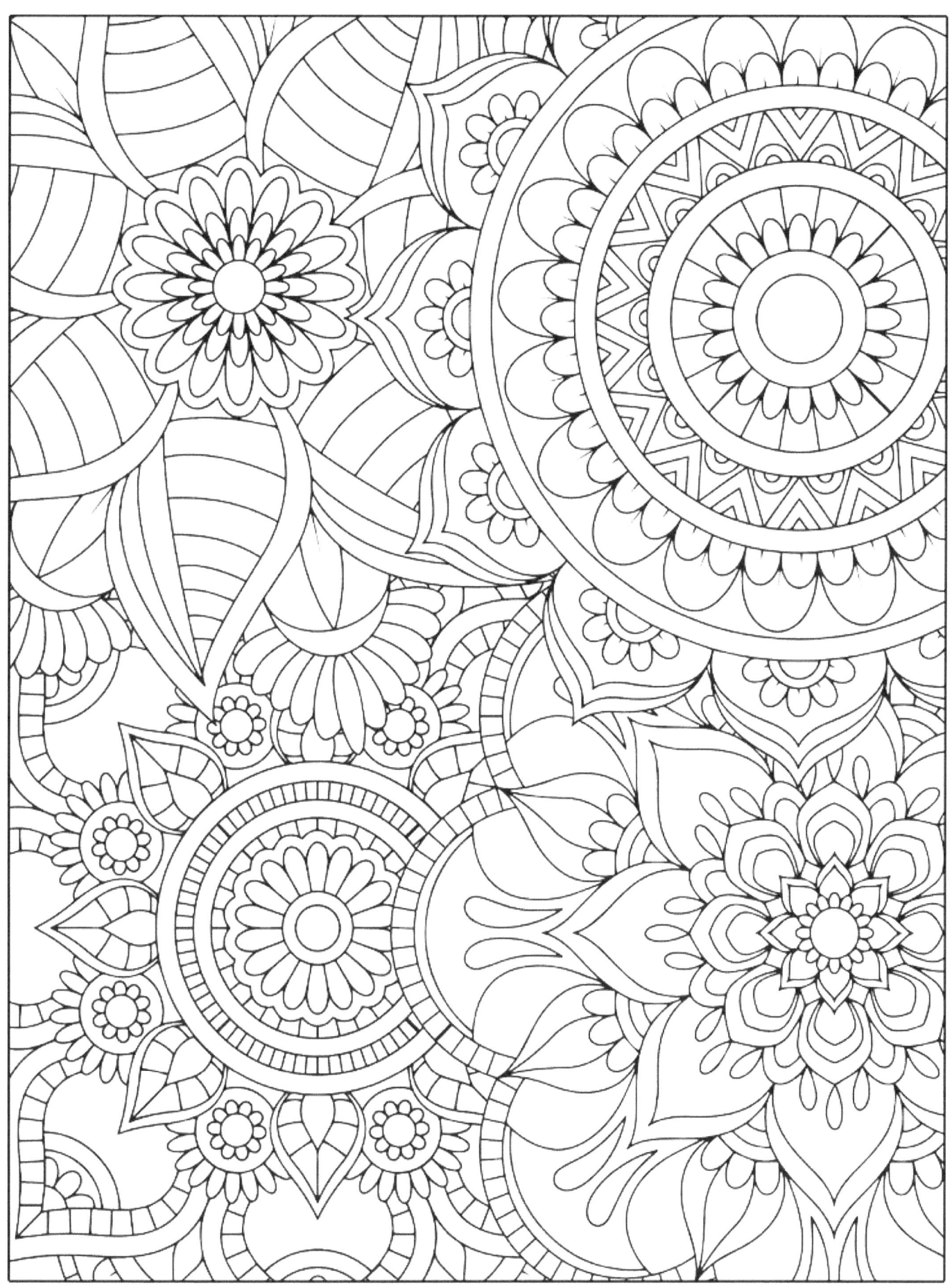

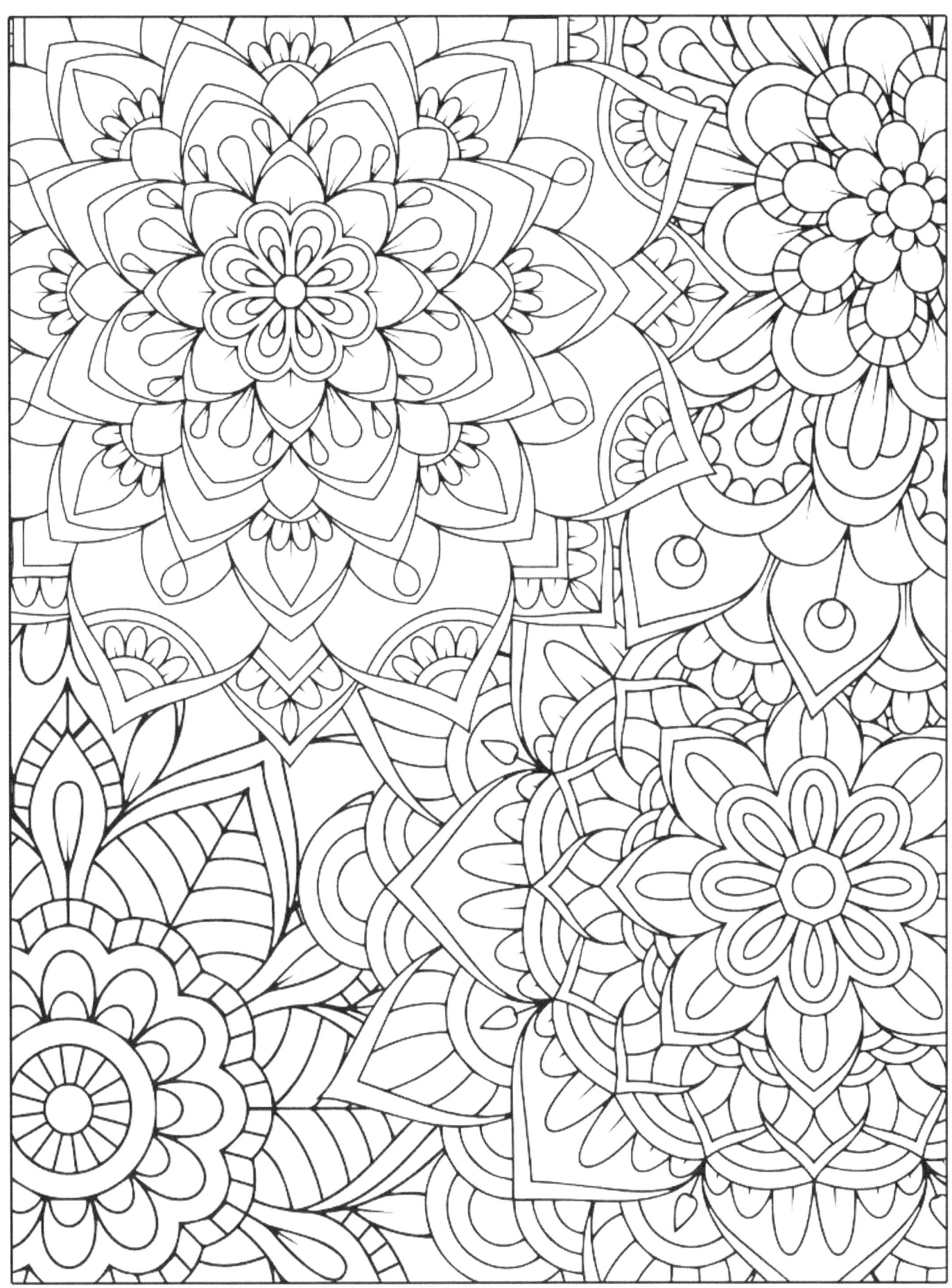

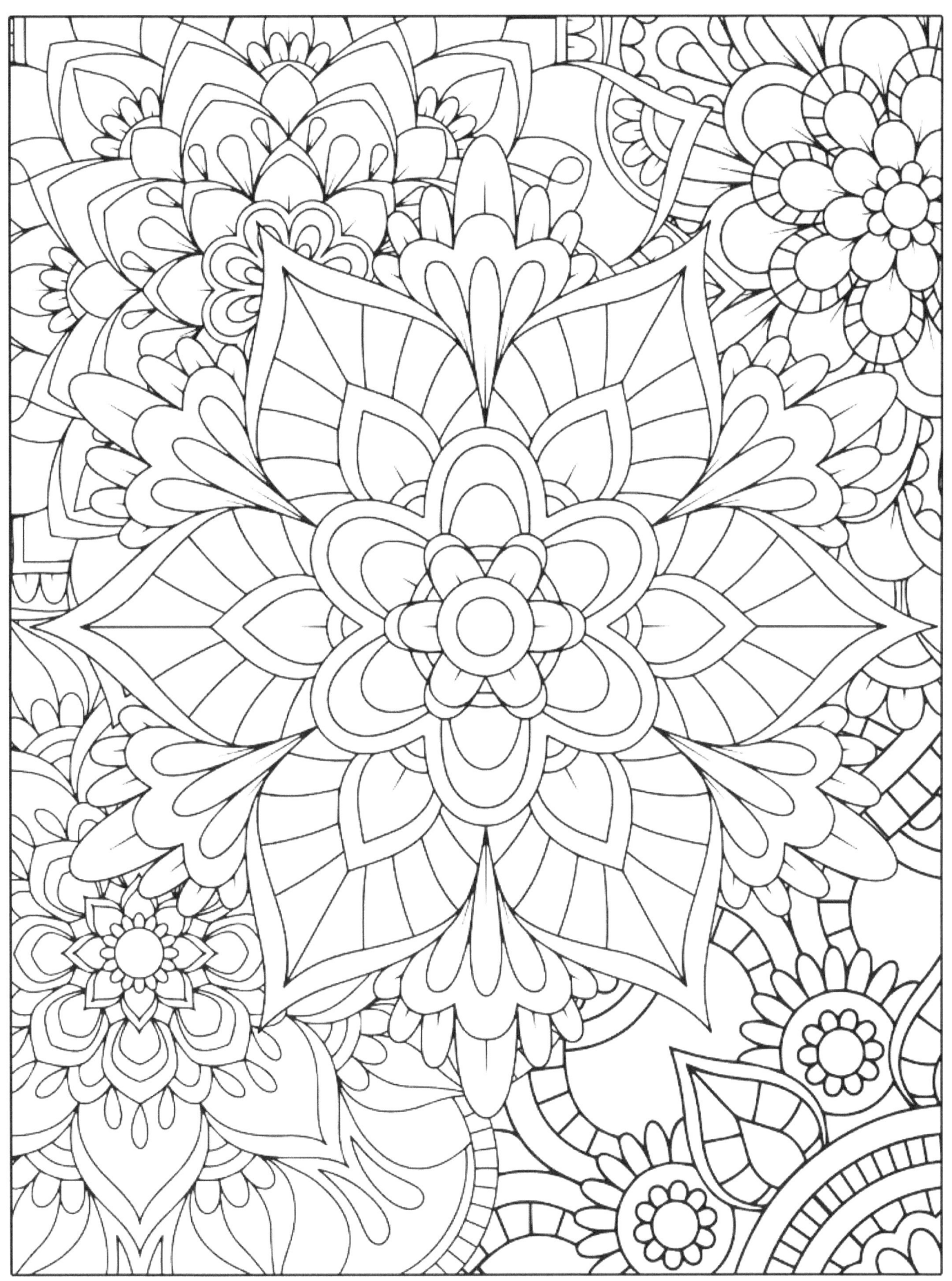

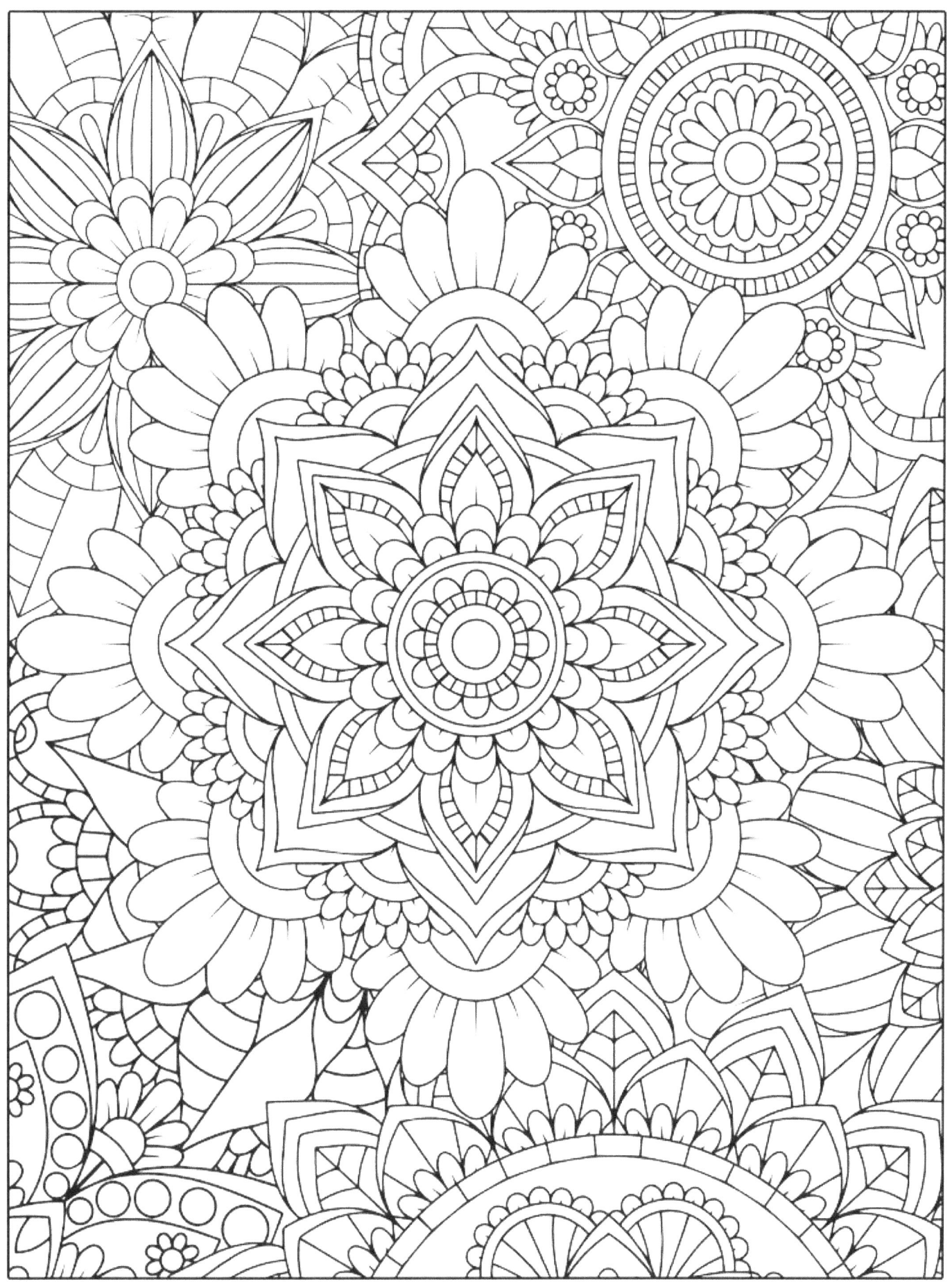

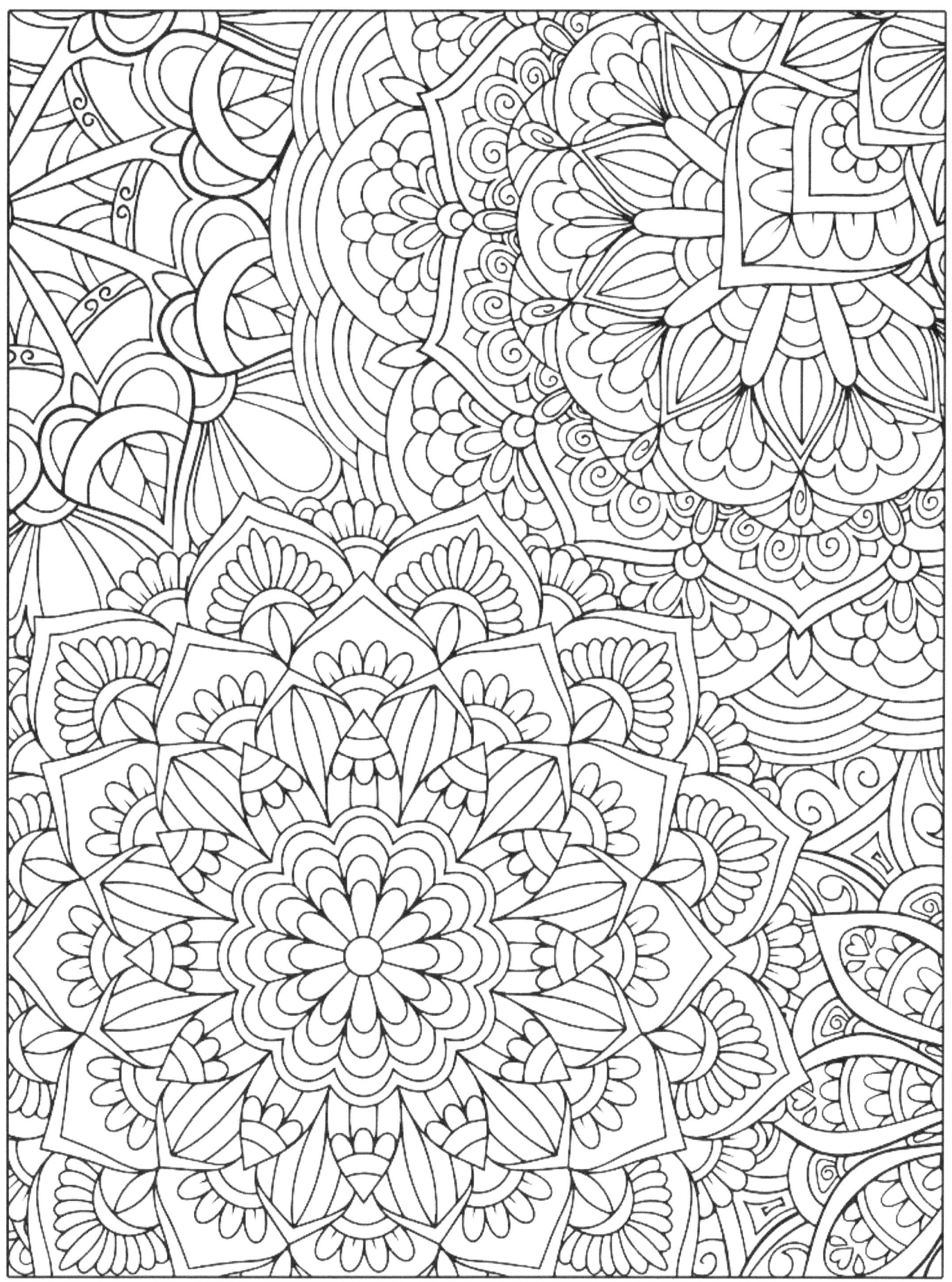

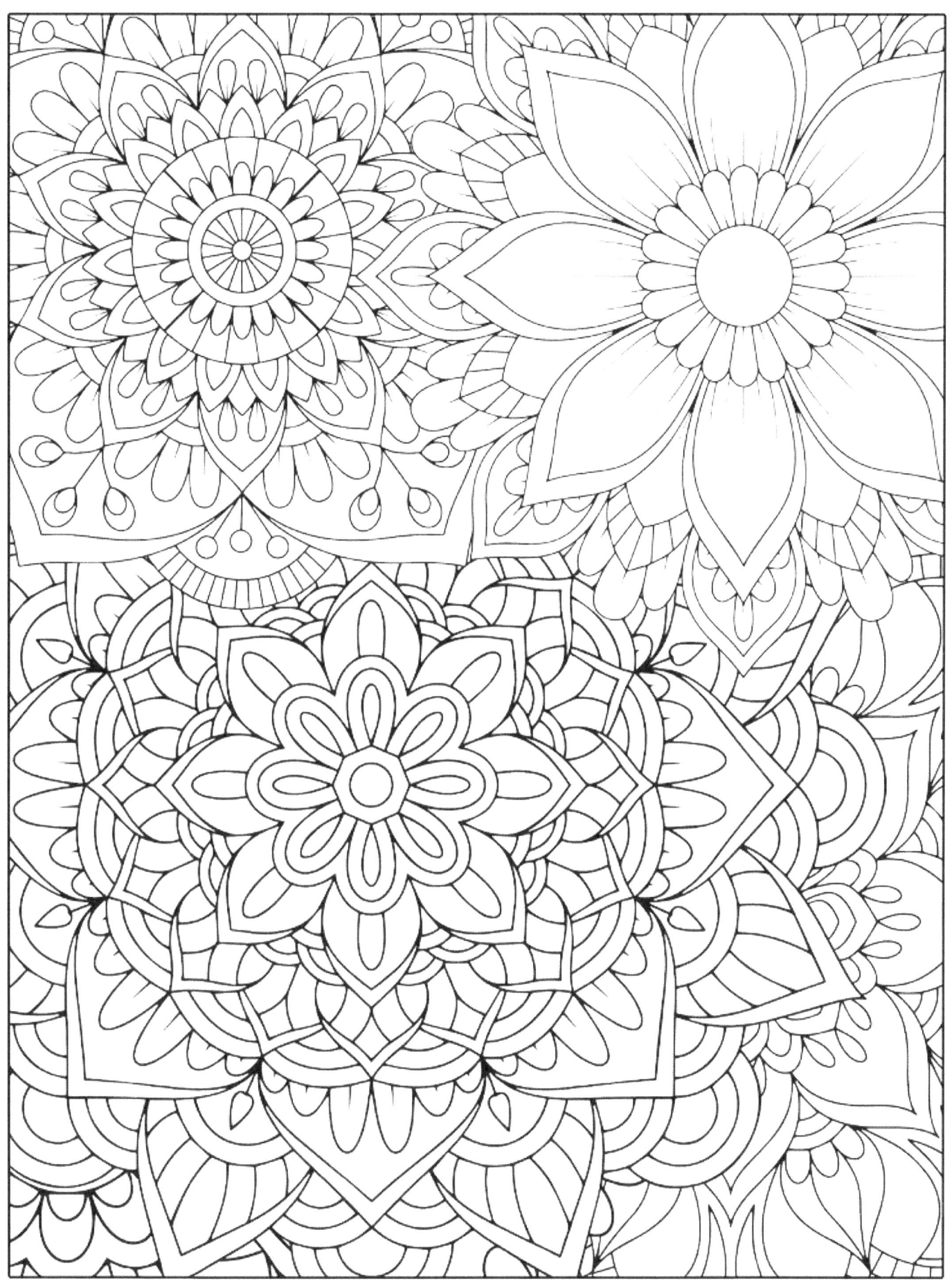

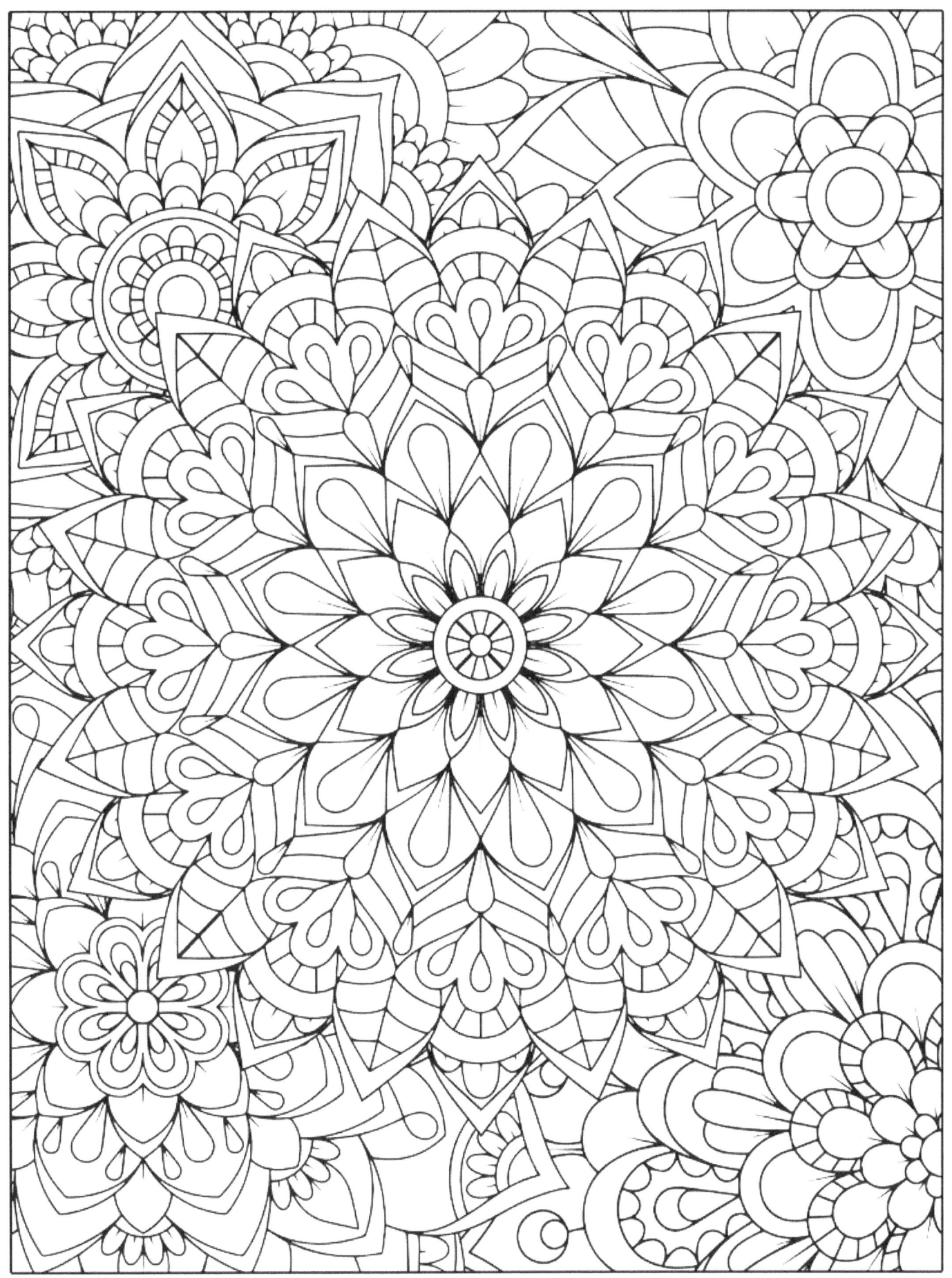

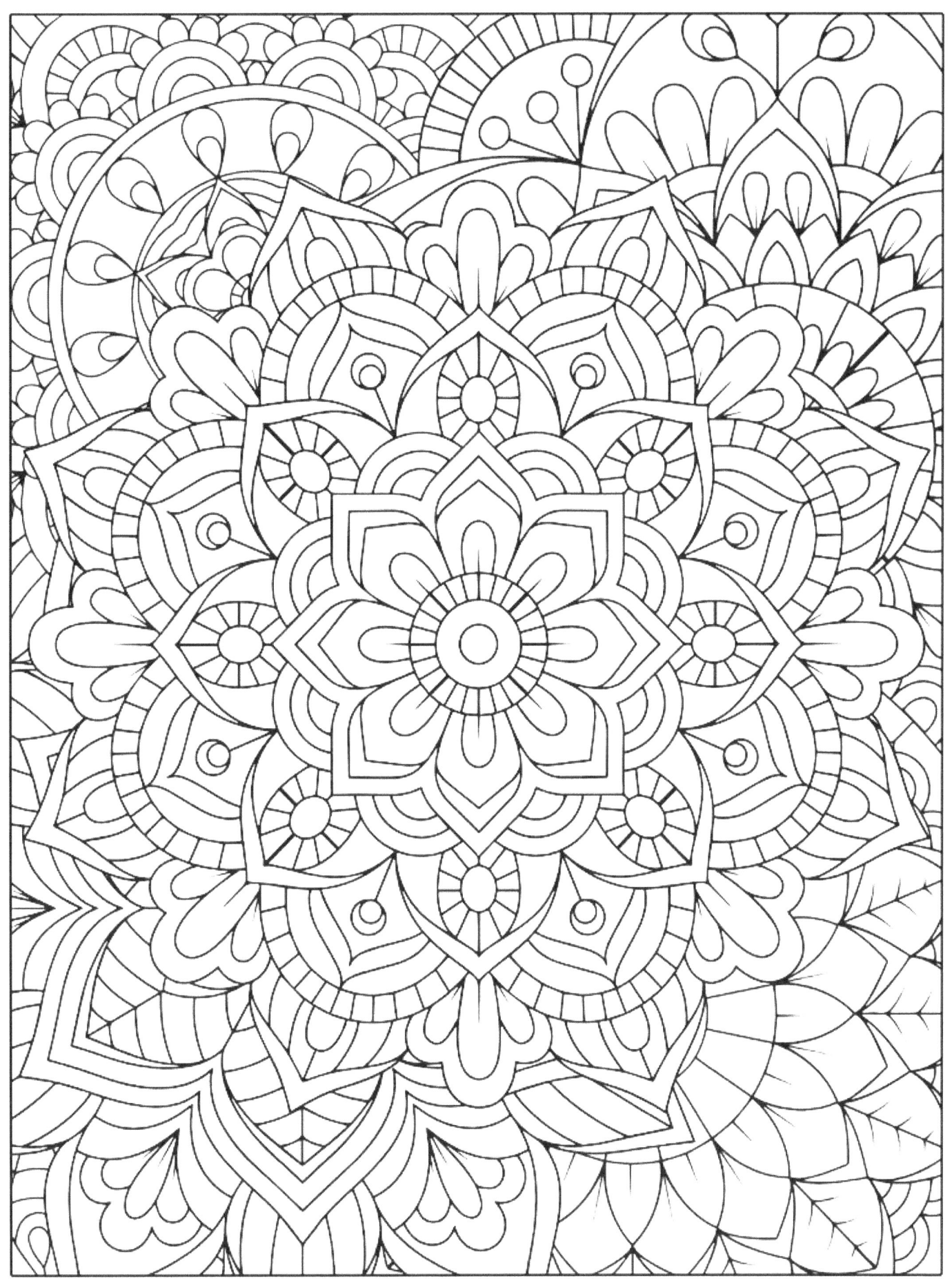

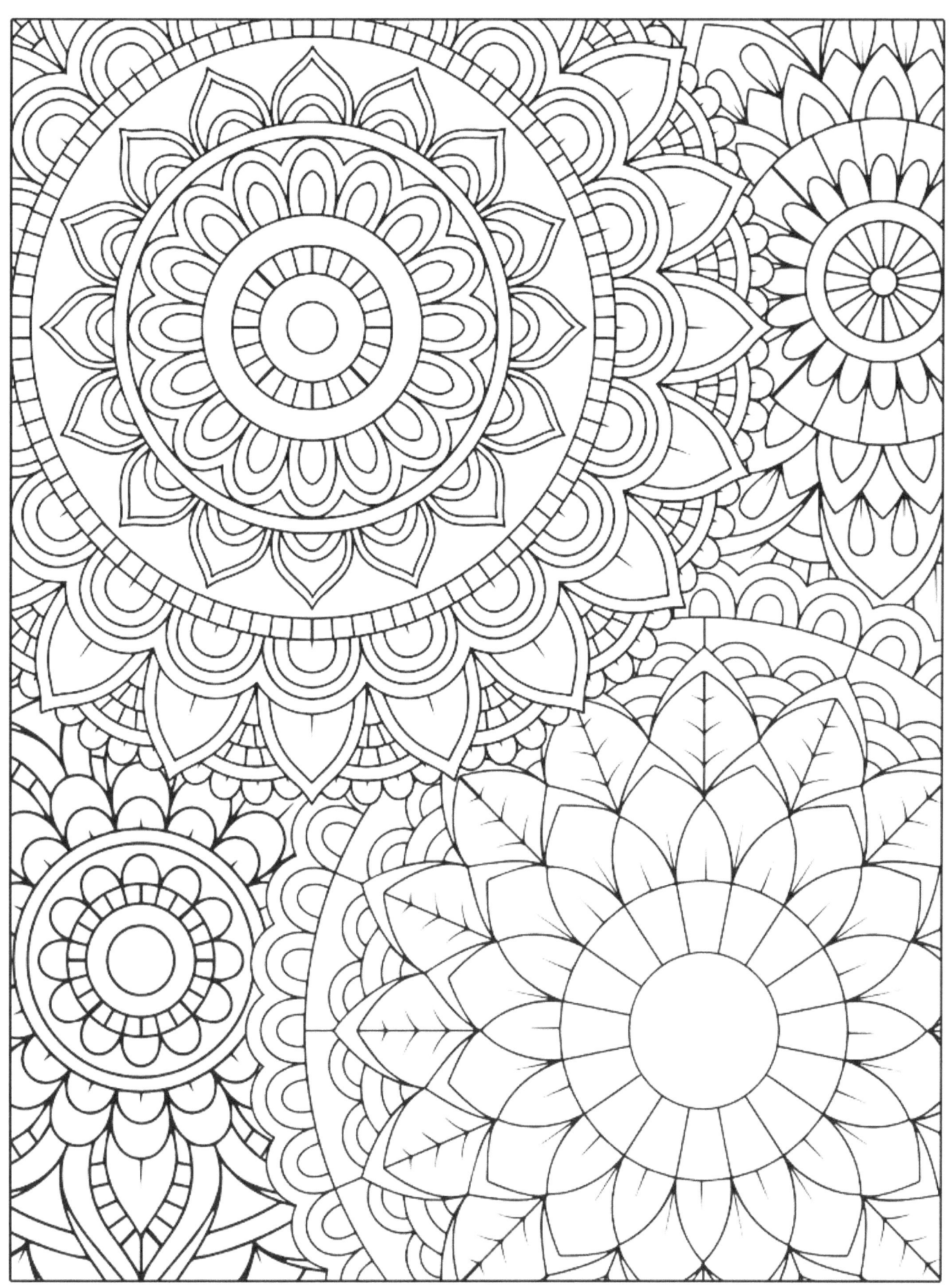

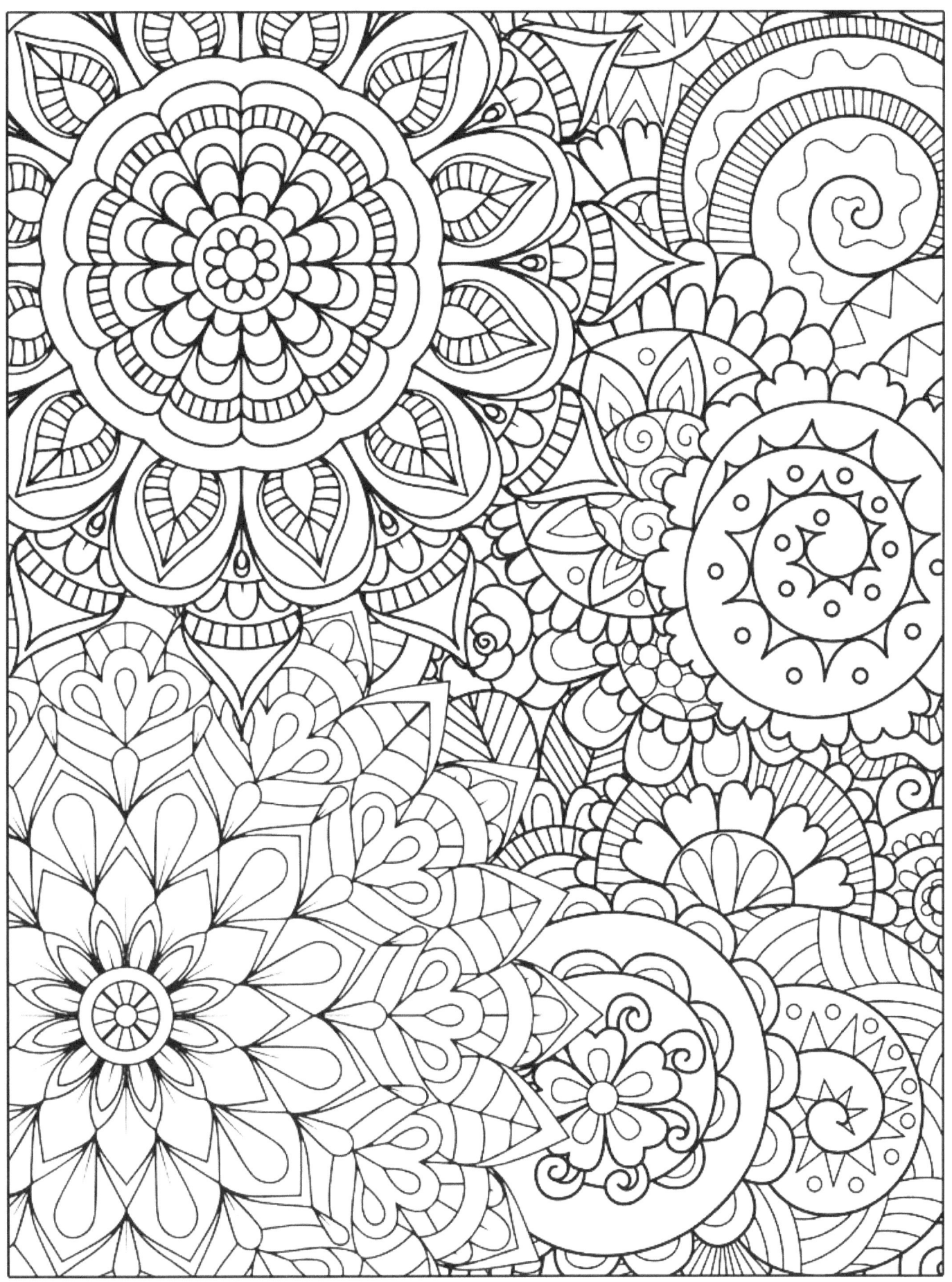

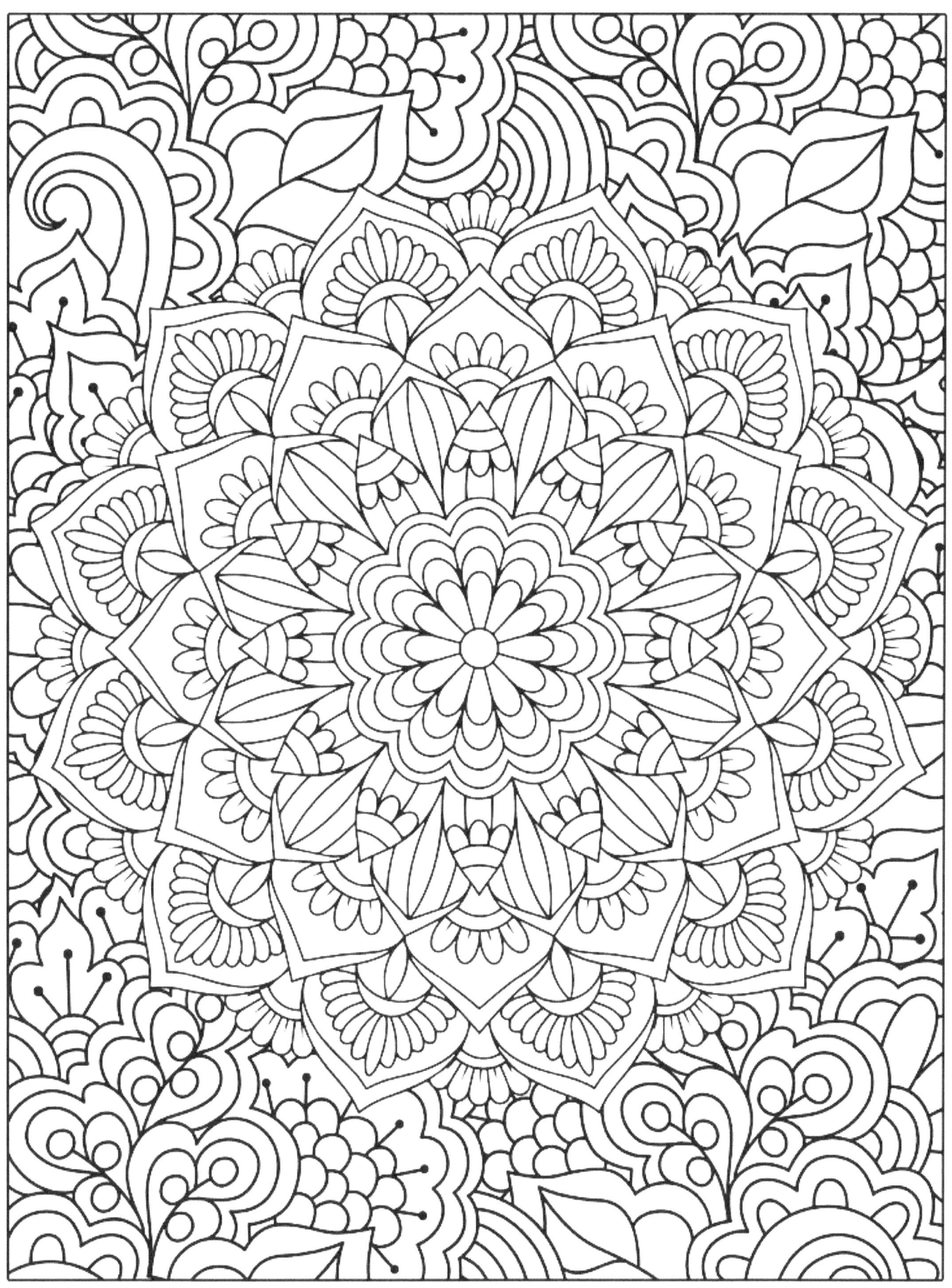

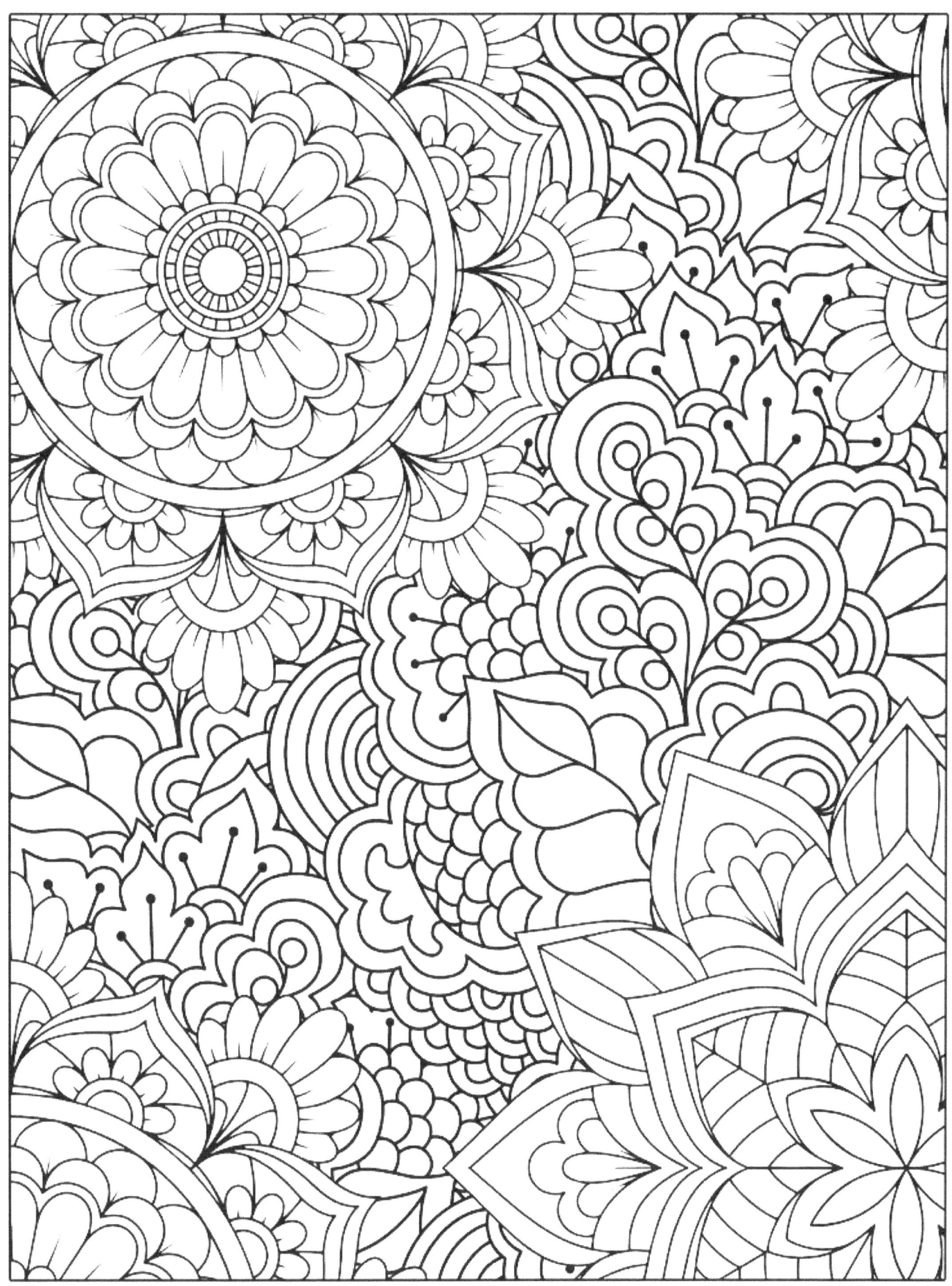

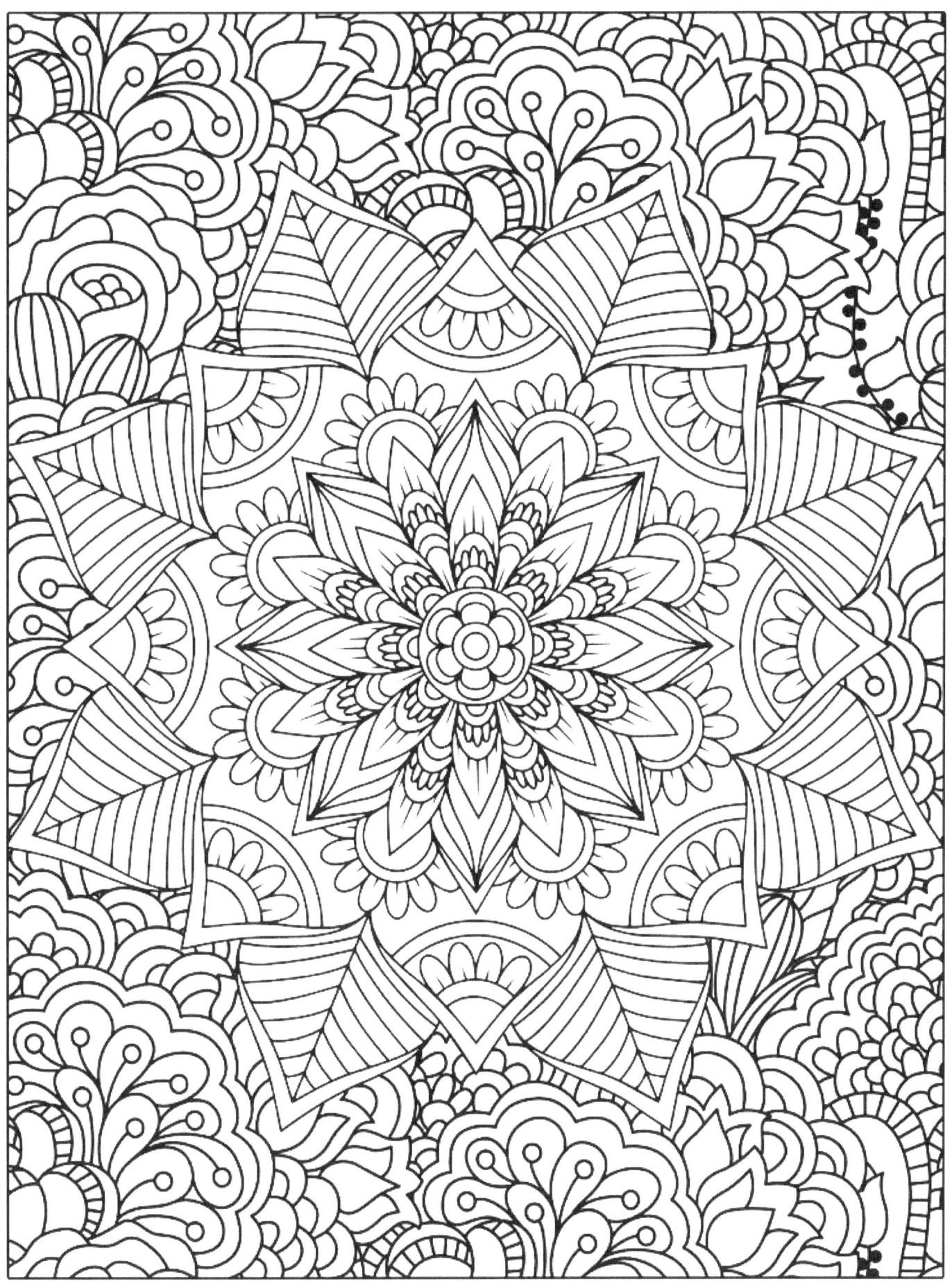

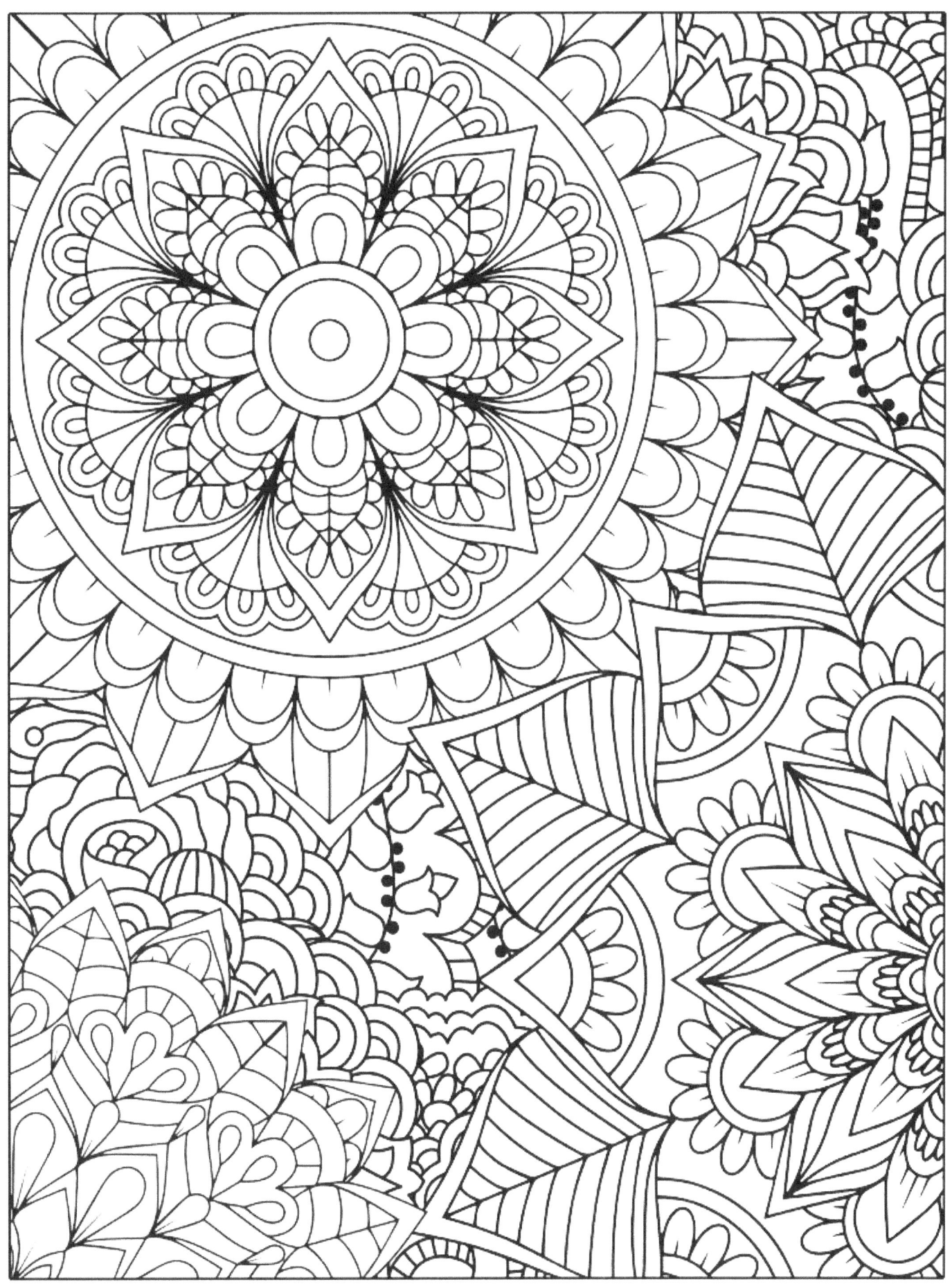

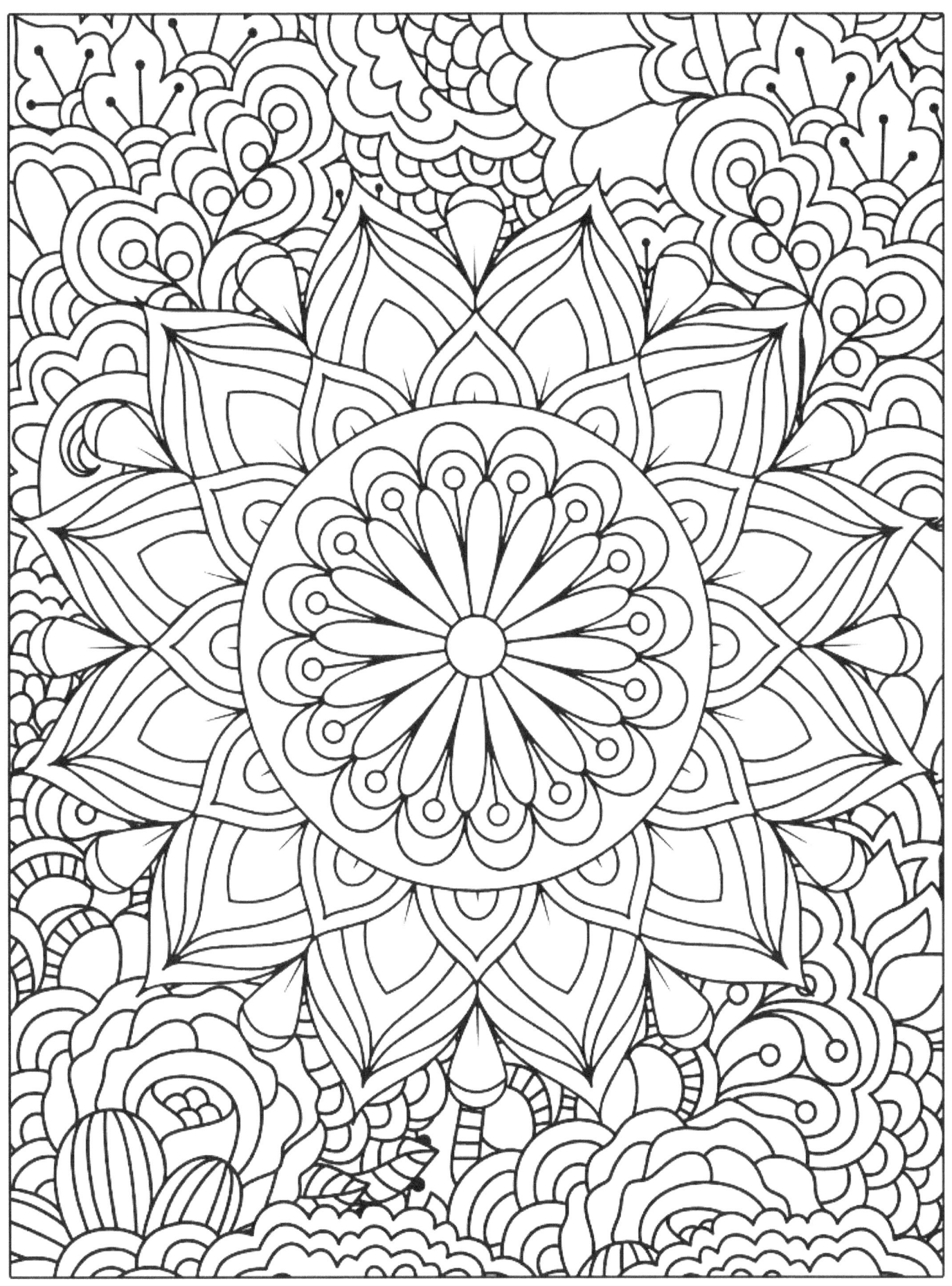

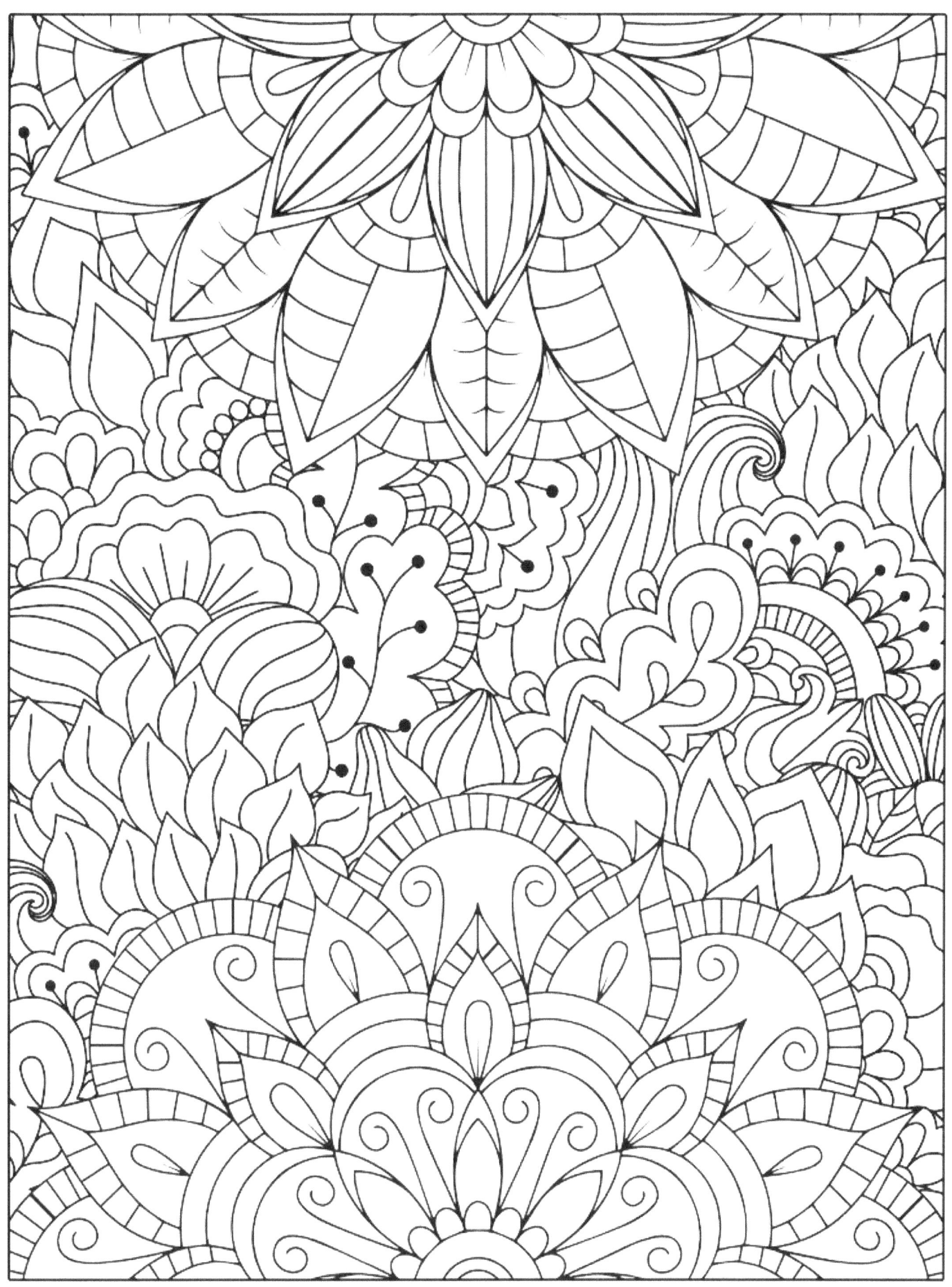

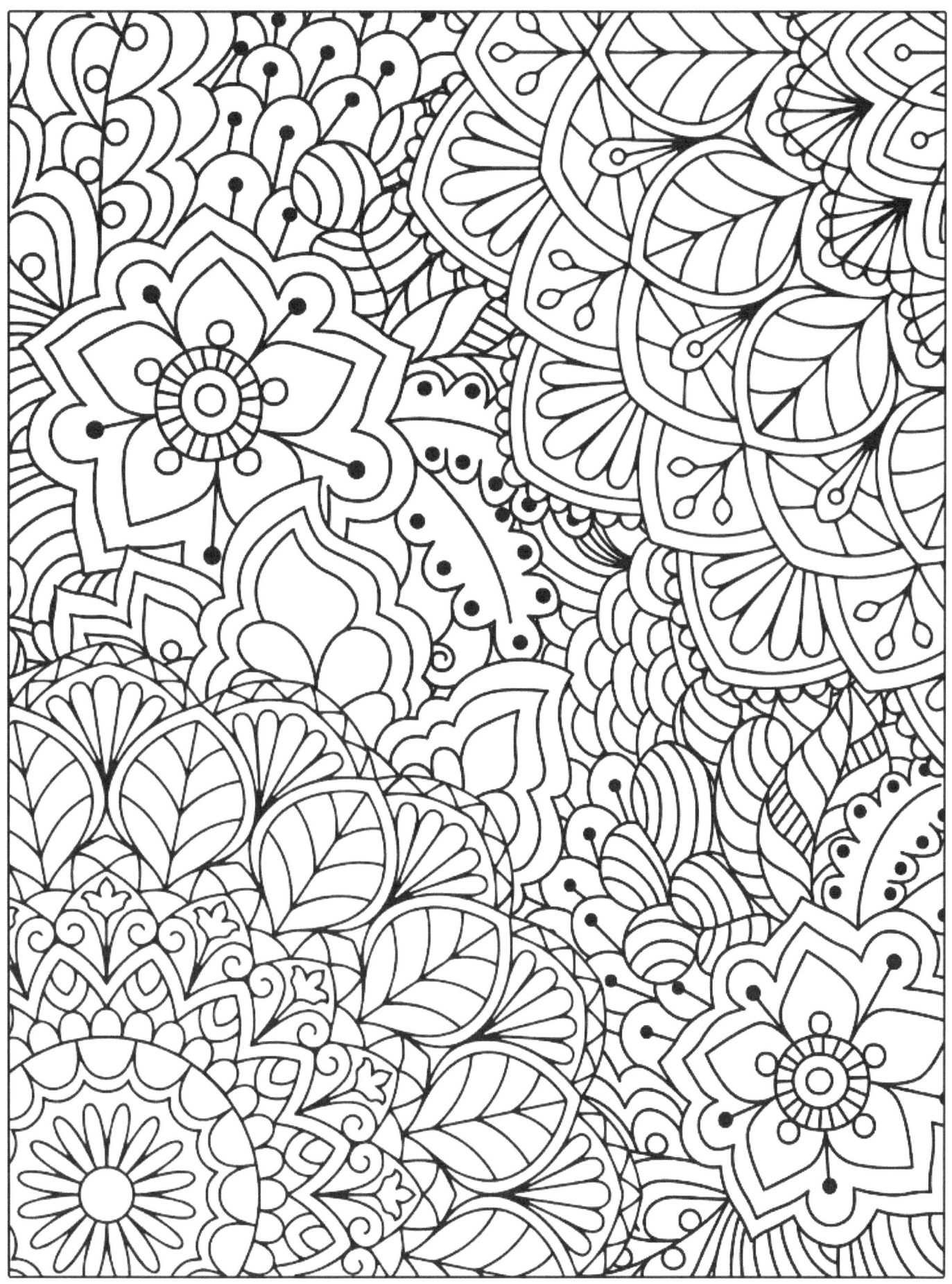

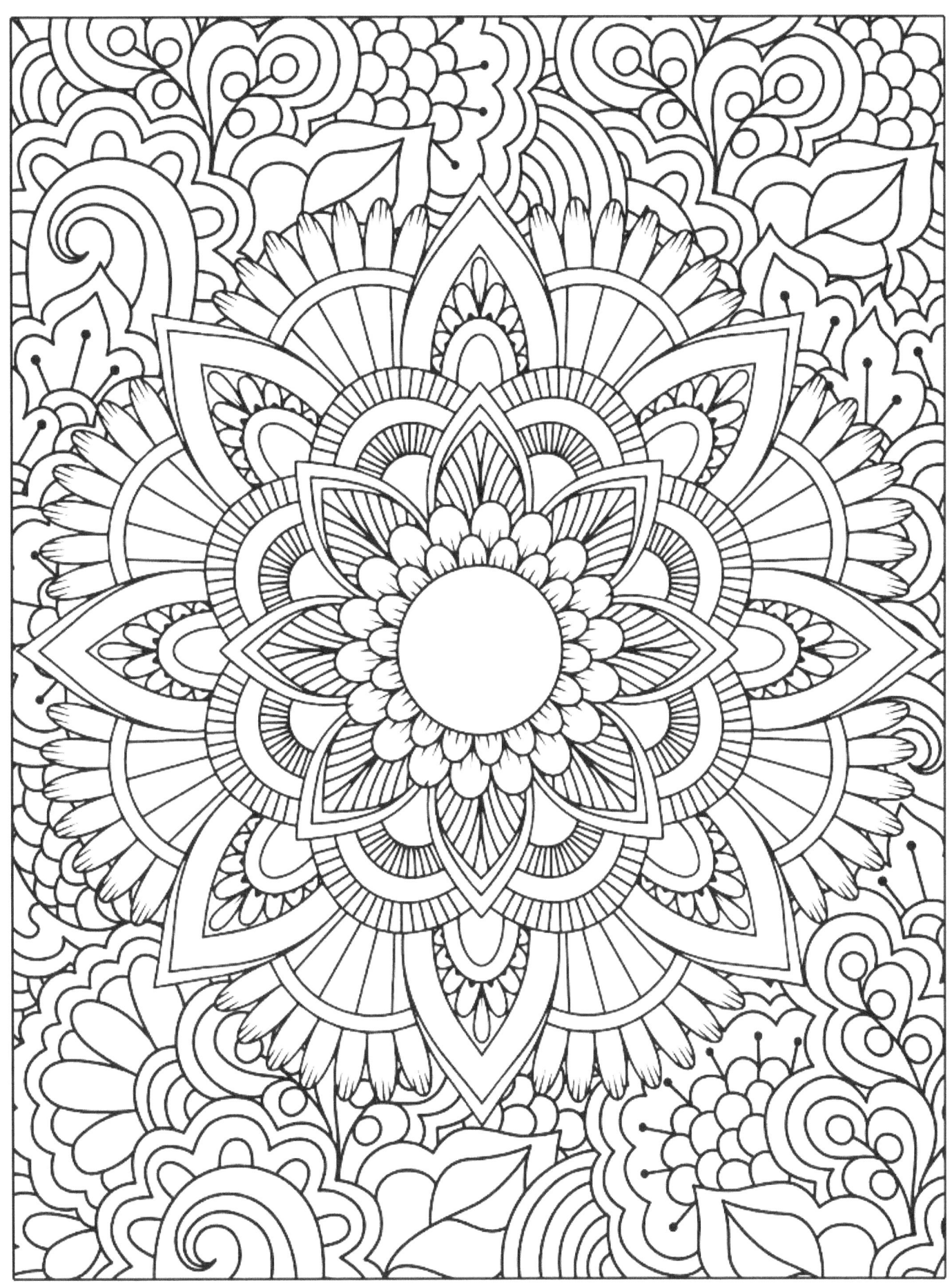

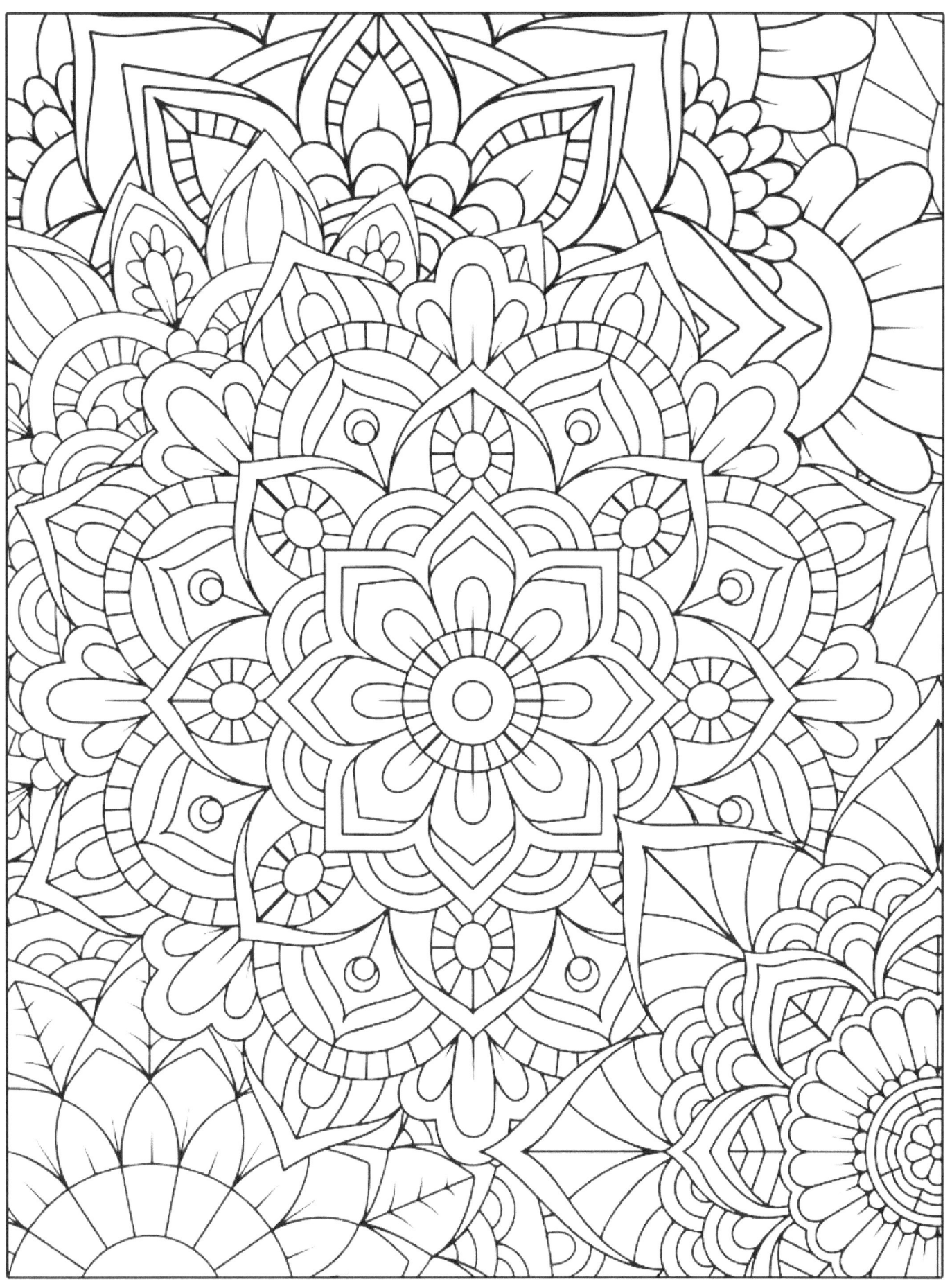

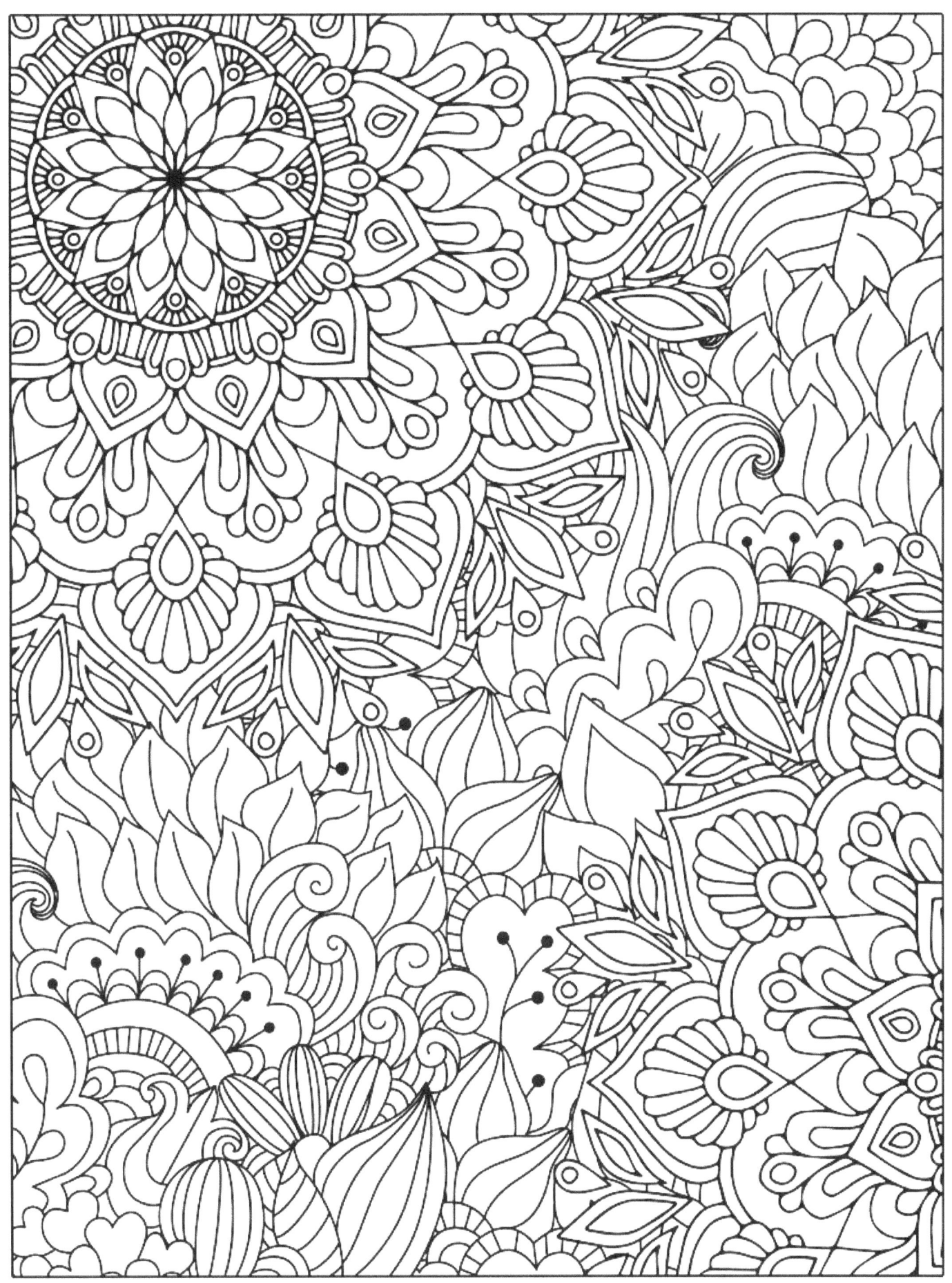

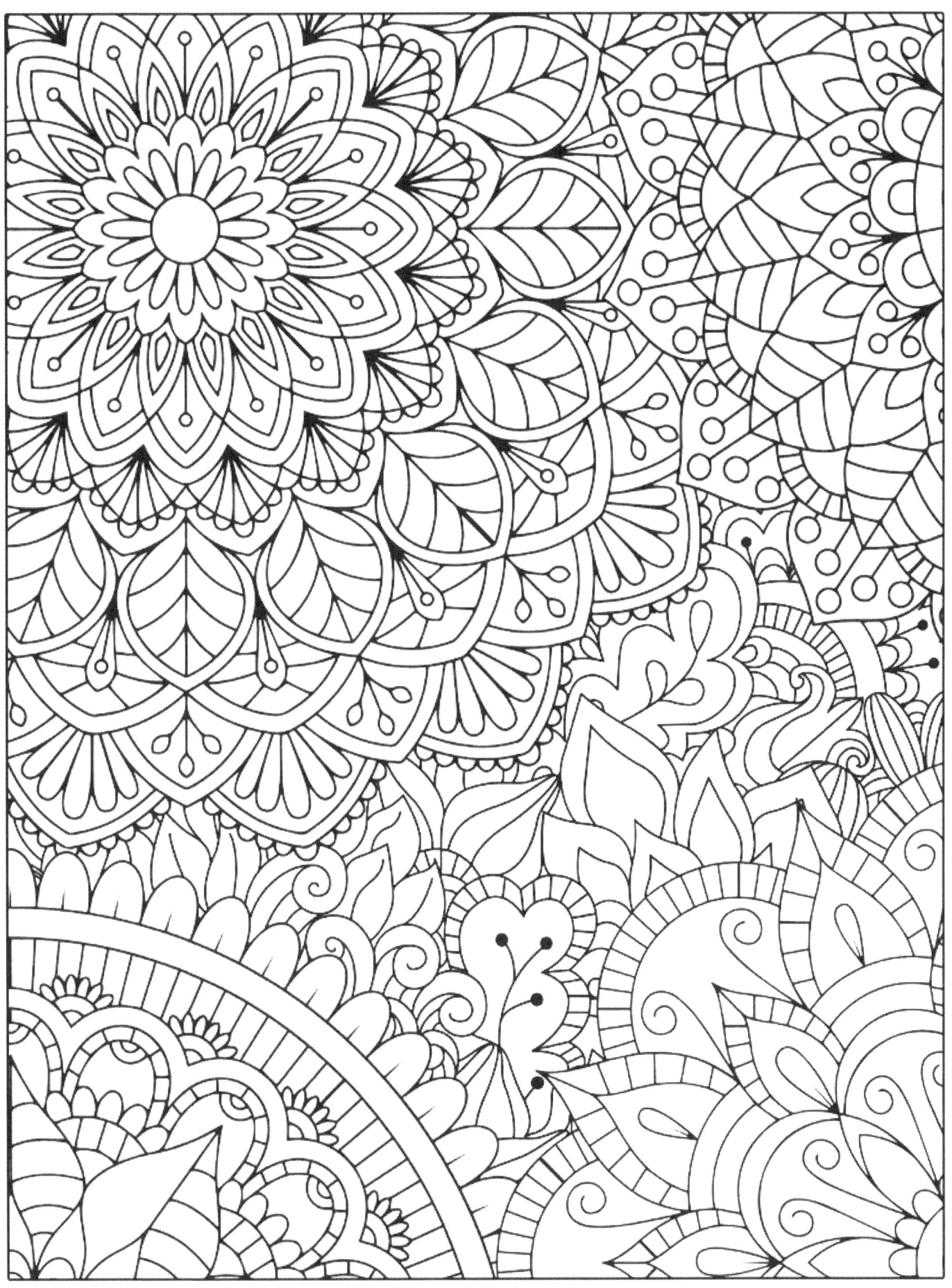

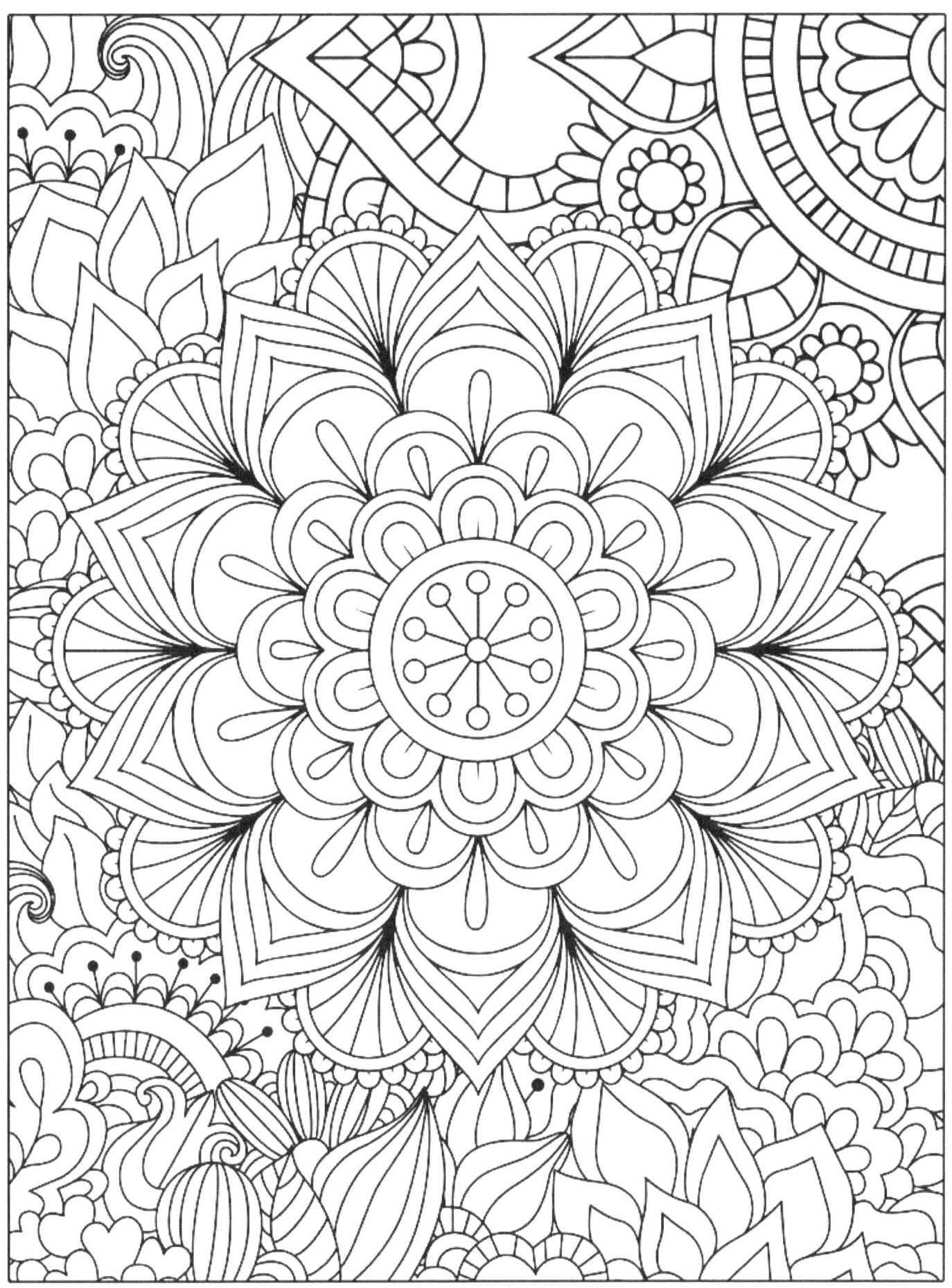

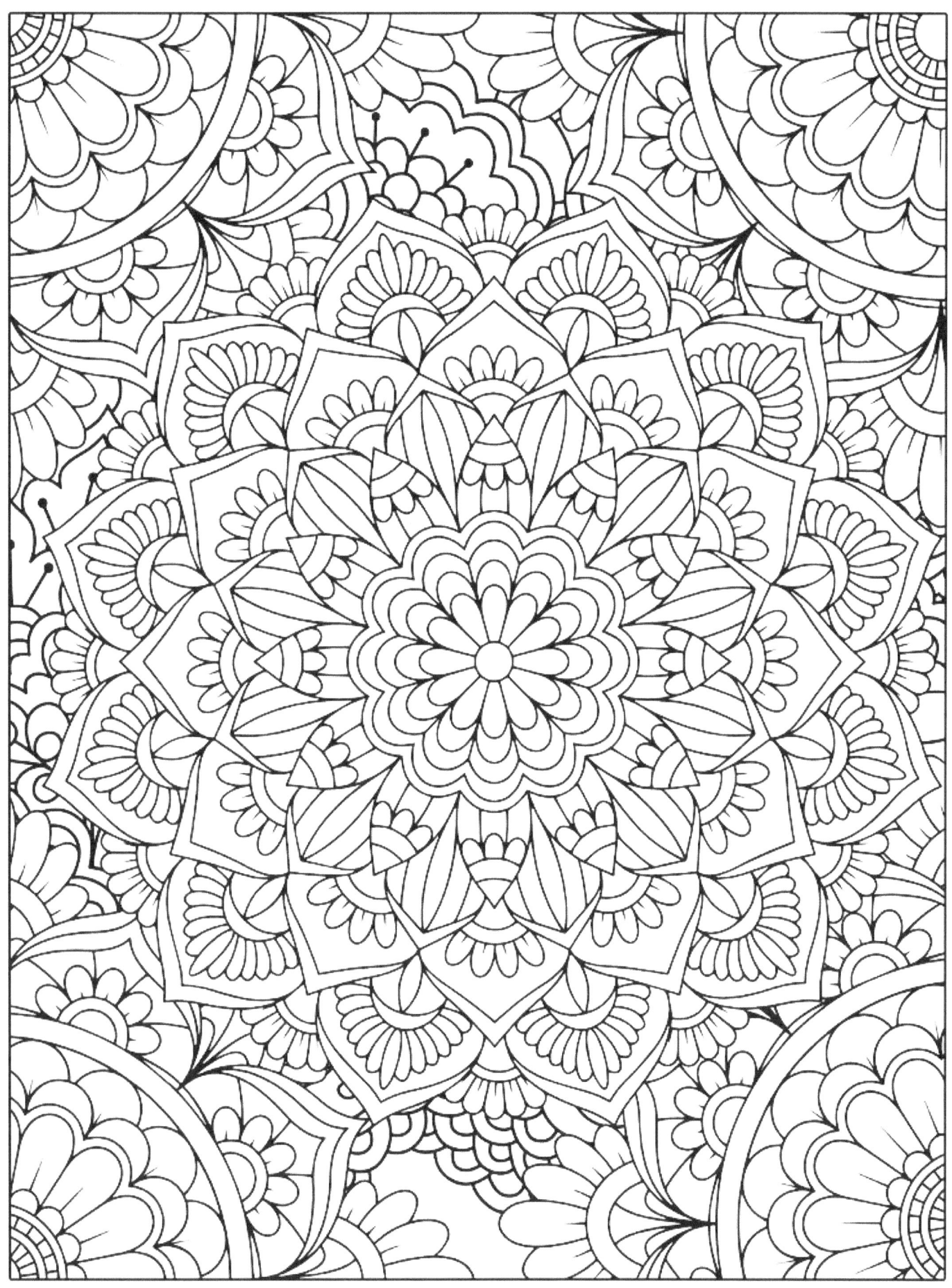

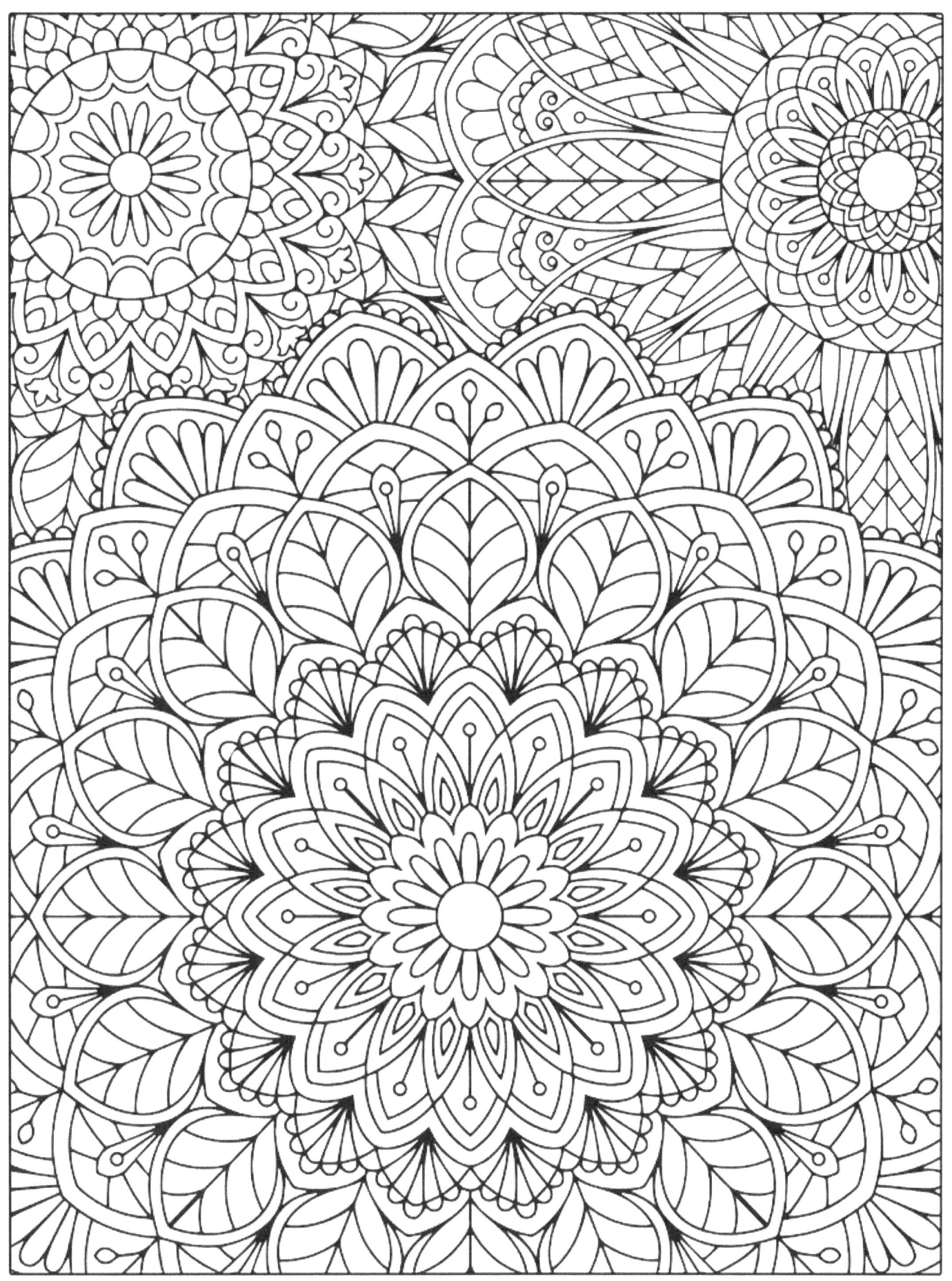

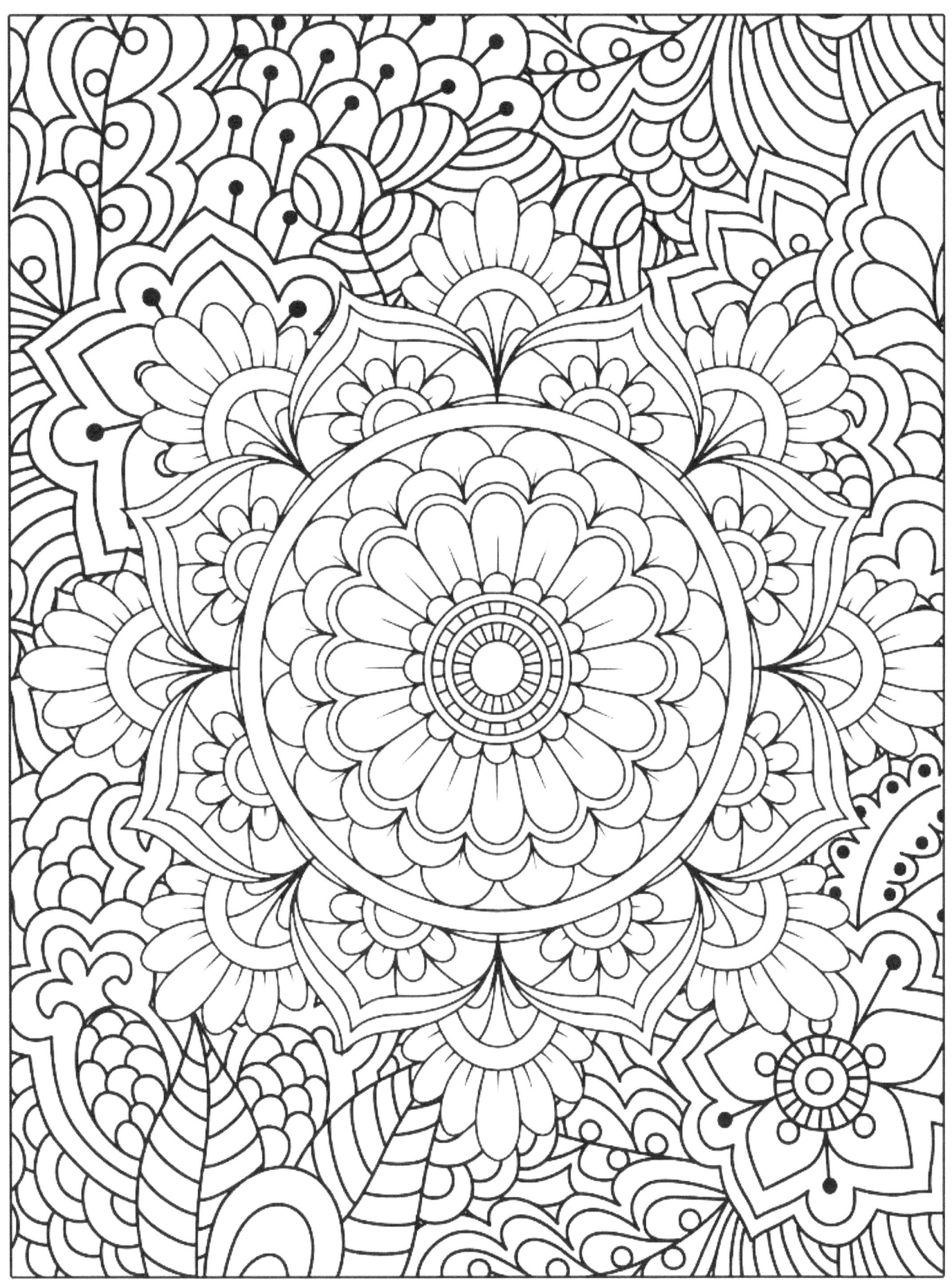

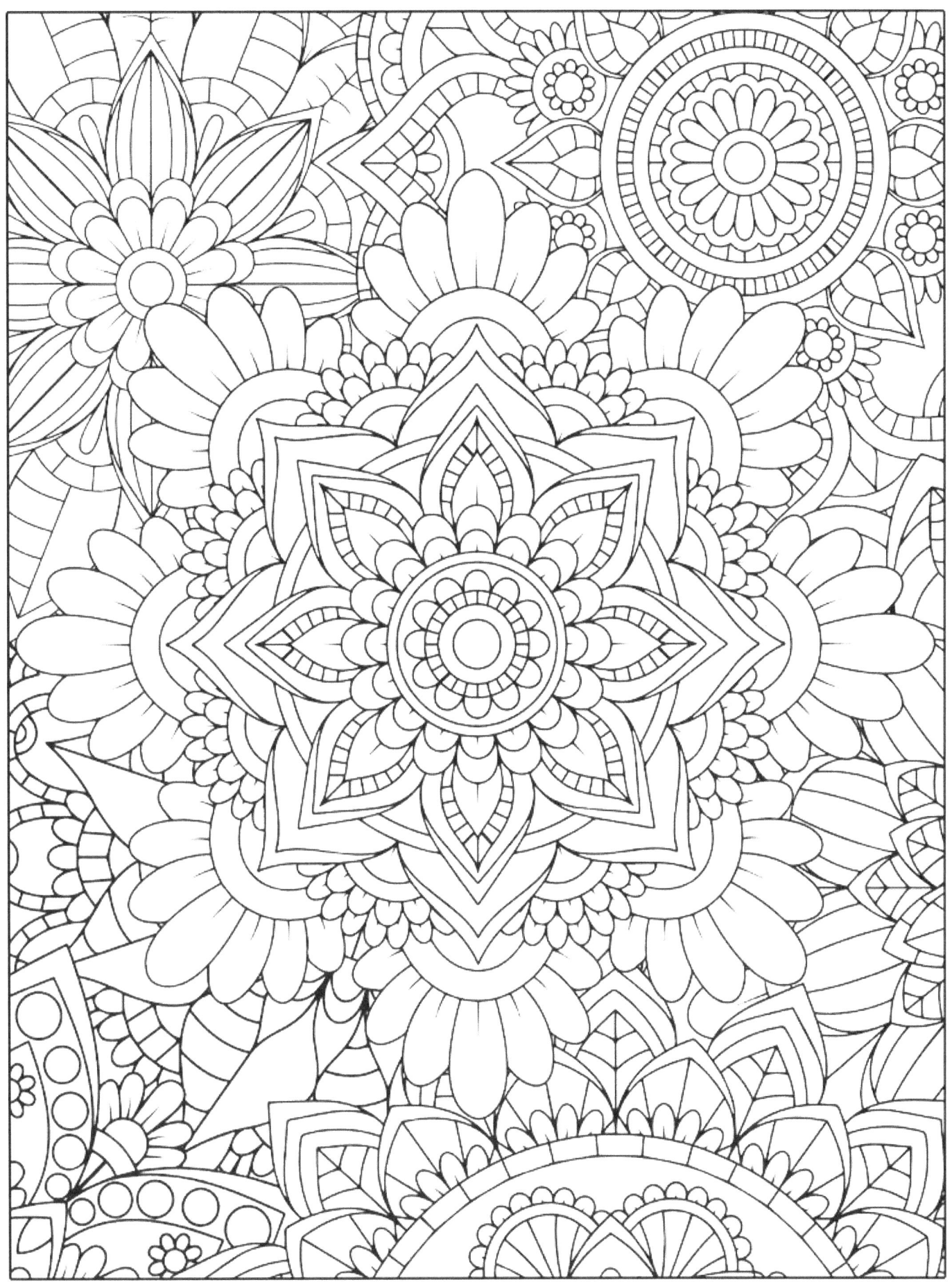

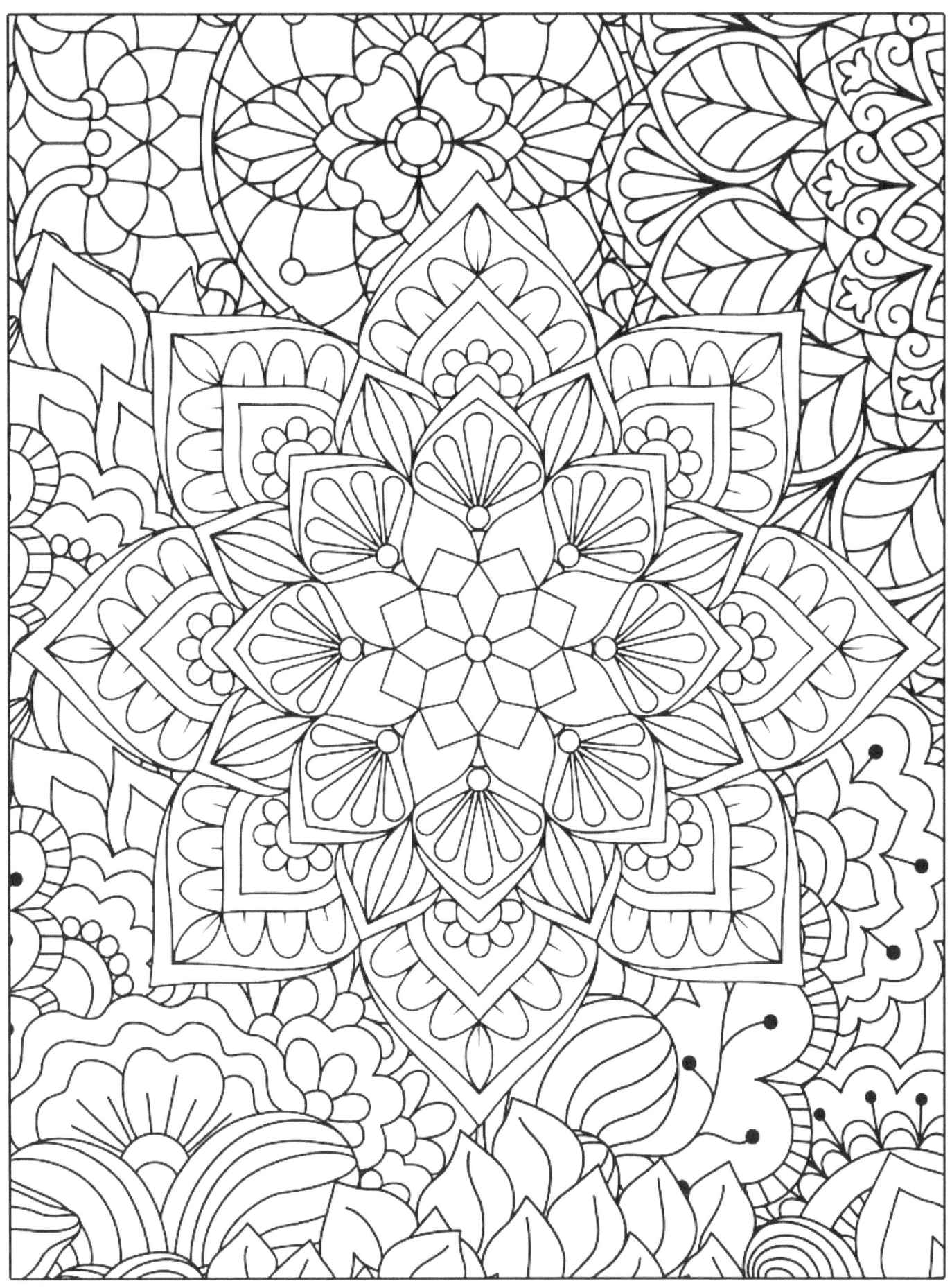

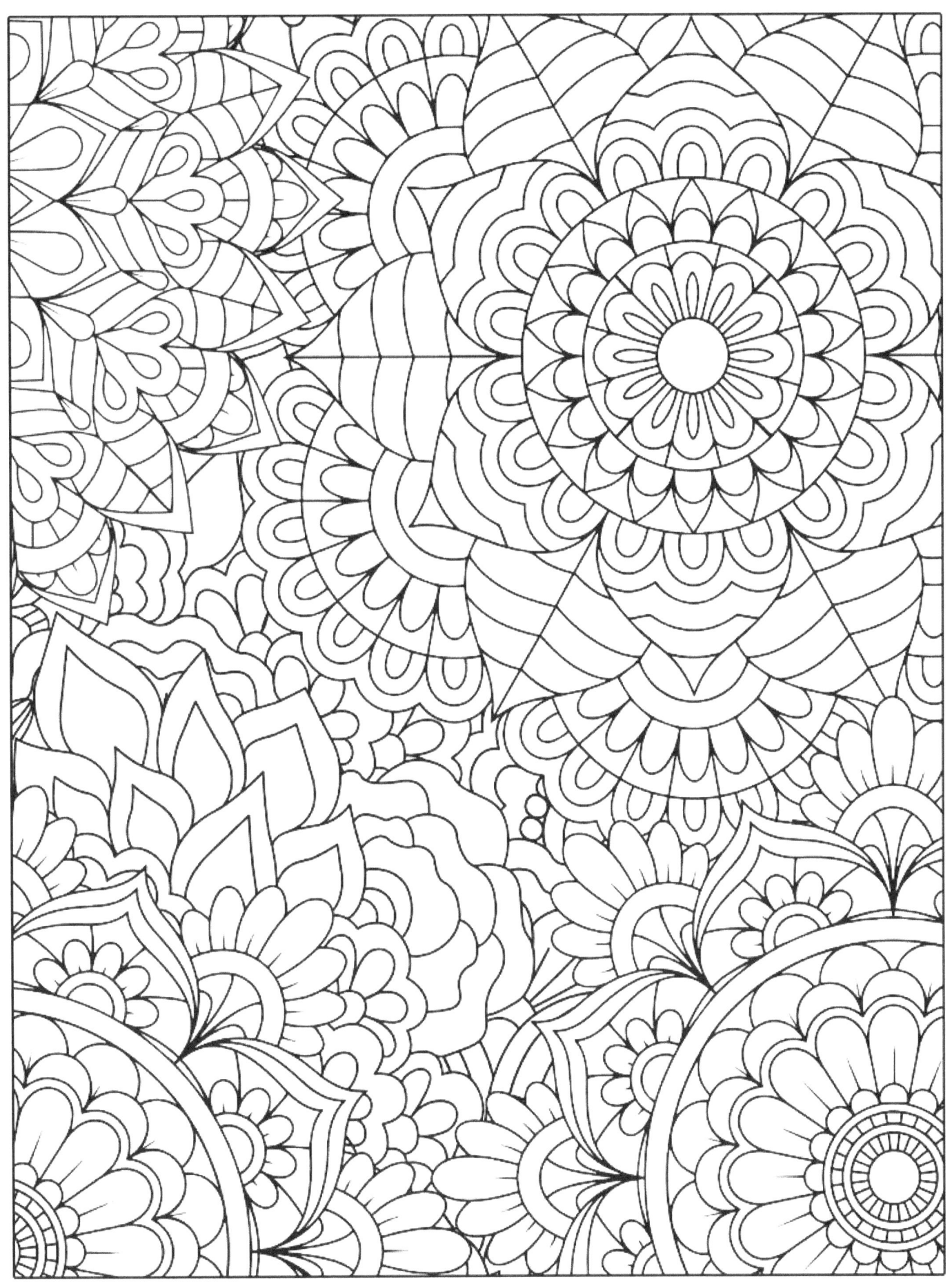

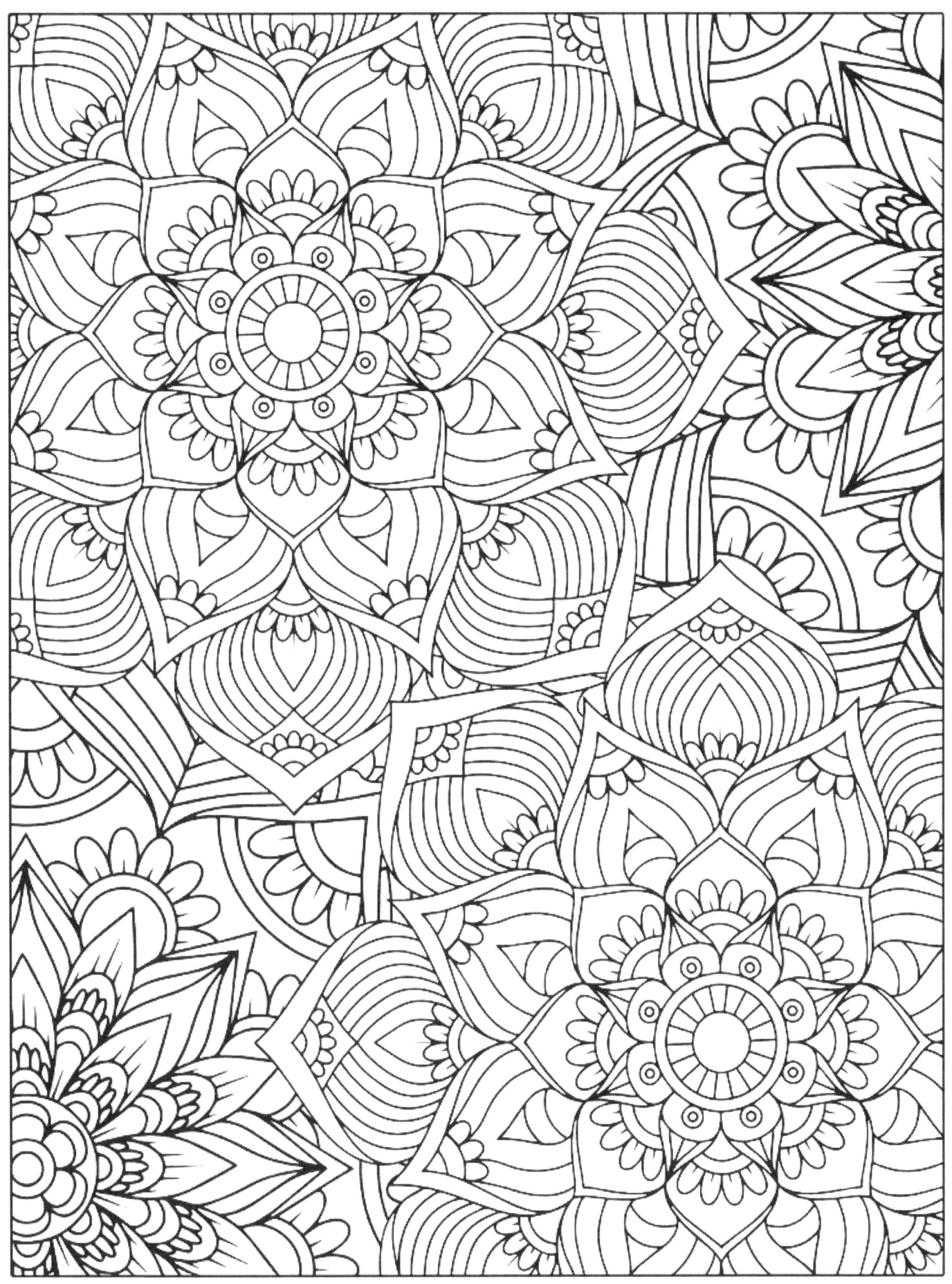

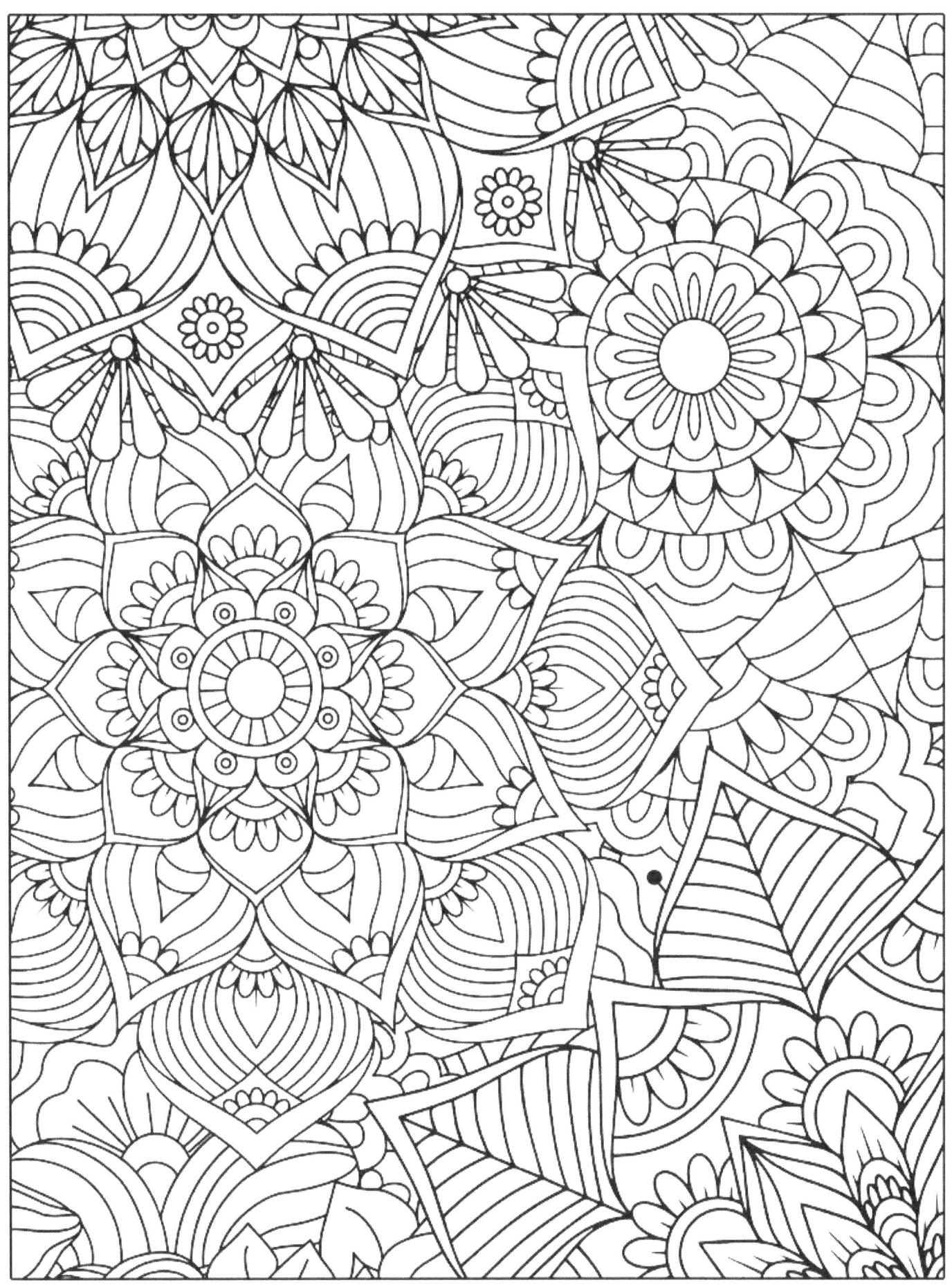

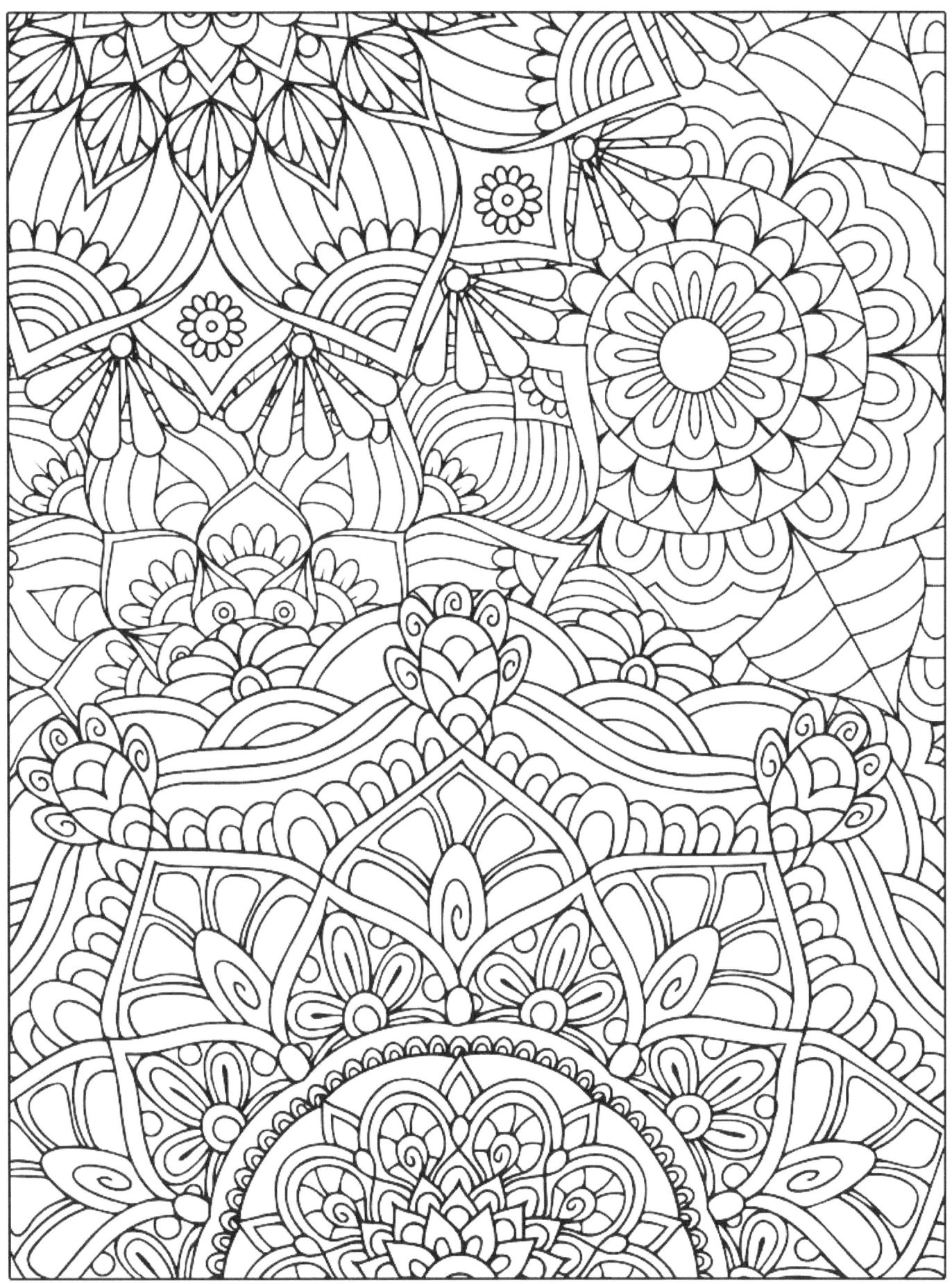

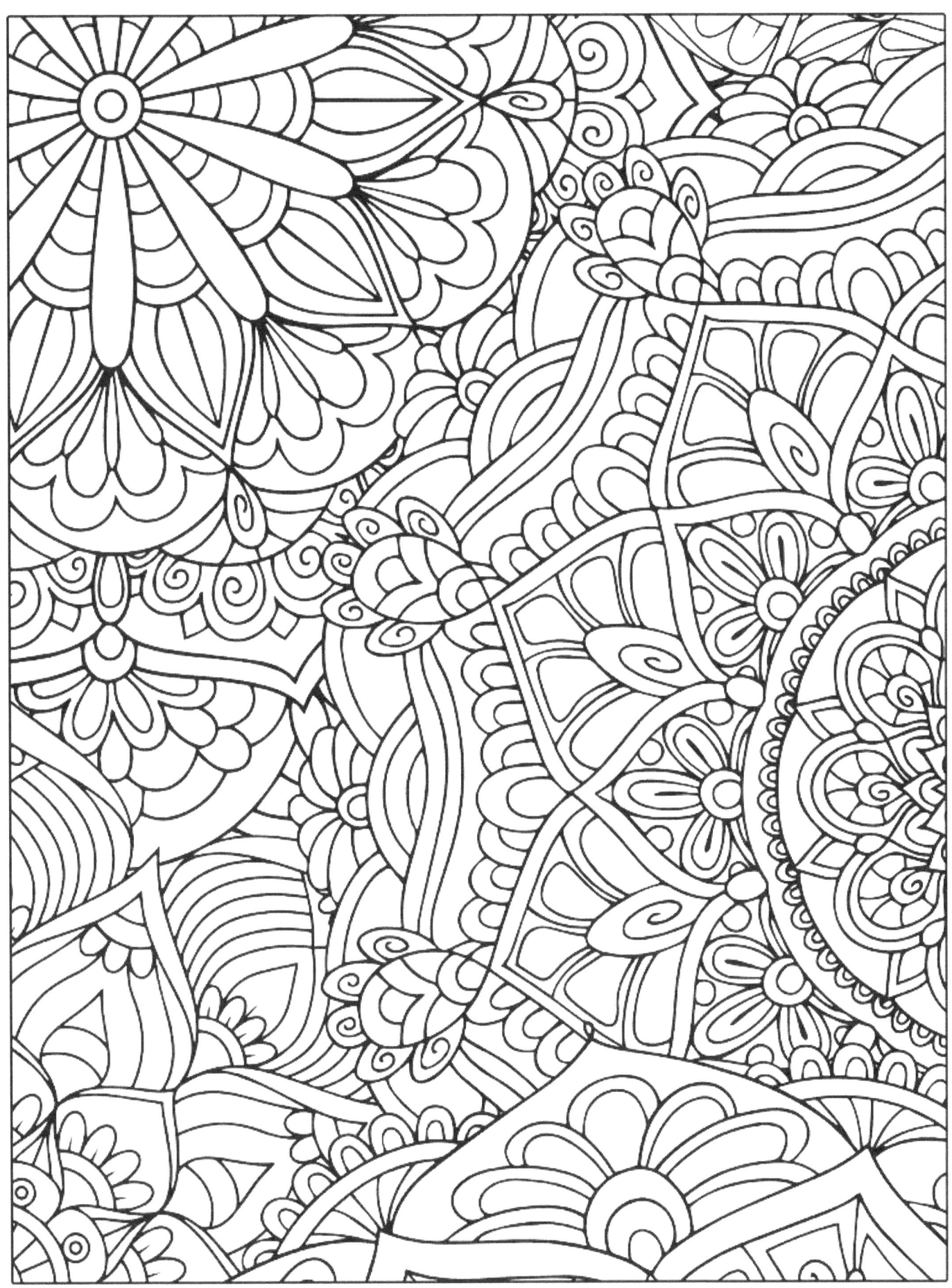

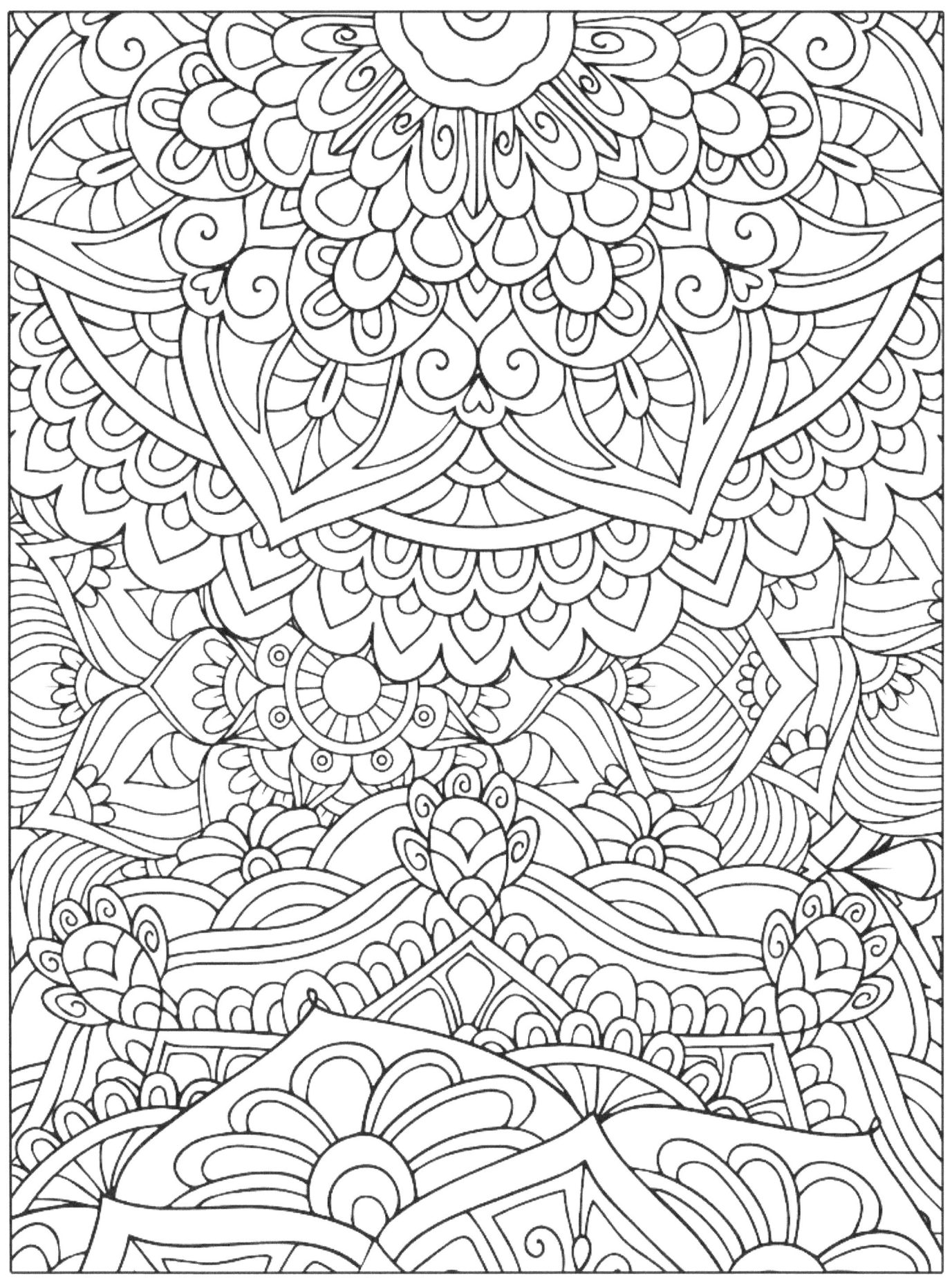

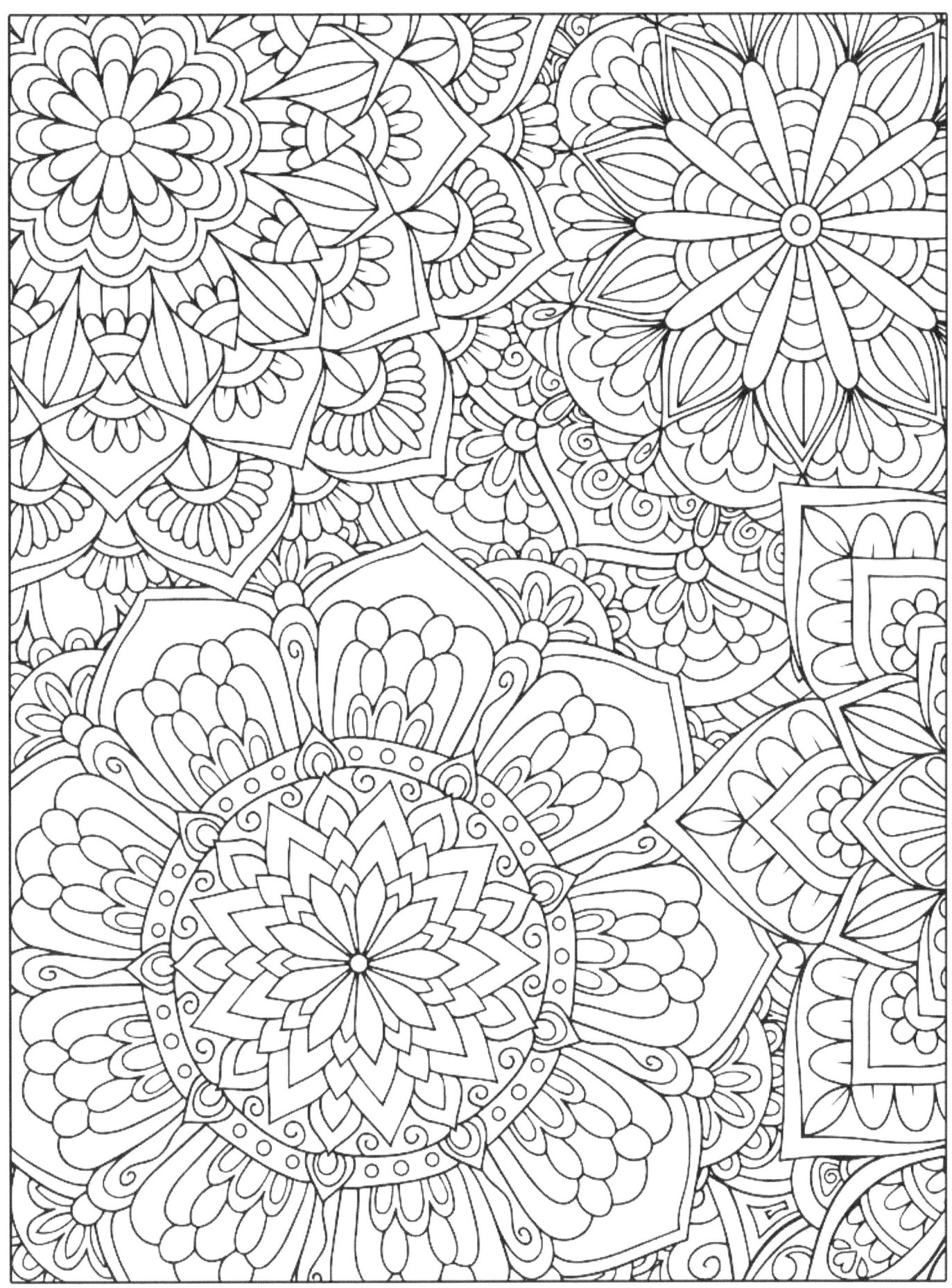

www.ingramcontent.com/pod-product-compliance
Lightning Source LLC
Chambersburg PA
CBHW080842220526
45467CB00008B/2355